CONSTELLATIONS WITHIN

Stories and Practices from 27 Lunar Mansions to Empower You

Nitin Vasishtha

Mining Wisdom

Book Title: Constellations Within: Stories and Practices from 27 Lunar Mansions to Empower You
Author: Nitin Vasishtha

Published by: Mining Wisdom
An imprint of Vedology Consulting (OPC) Pvt. Ltd.
33, NCC Urban Green Province, Sarjapur
Bengaluru, 562125, India
https://www.miningwisdom.com/

ISBN:978-81-980529-2-6(hardcover)
ISBN: 978-81-980529-9-5 (paperback)
ISBN: 978-81-980529-0-2 (ebook)
First Edition: [2024]
Cover Design: Original design generated using DALL-E, extensively modified by Nitin Umanath Dubey
Interior Design: Nitin Umanath Dubey
For inquiries, contact: nitin.vasishtha@miningwisdom.com

Homage to My Ancestors and Parents

I offer my deepest gratitude to my ancestors, beginning with Sage Vasishtha and his wife Devi Arundhati, and the legacy of this lineage that instills in me a sense of humility and responsibility. I honor my ancestors by adopting his name as my pen name. I am eternally grateful to my parents, Smt. Suhasini Dubey and Shri Umanath Dubey, for their sacrifices that helped me with my education, values, and opportunities.

My salutations to Maa Saraswati, the operating system of the universe (and our minds). I merely wield the pen, it is she who guides me with thoughts and words. I do not take this for granted.

Disclaimer

This book does not promote blind faith, superstition, black magic, or any practices that compromise rational thinking or individual well-being.

The author does not endorse or recommend visiting unskilled or unqualified astrologers or mystics. On the contrary, the narrative actively emphasizes personal reflection, critical thinking, and responsible decision-making as pathways to growth and clarity.

Astrology, like human beings, is complex. No single planet or constellation can define an individual's personality, fate or journey. Readers are encouraged to approach the concepts and ideas presented in this book with an open mind, balanced skepticism, and a focus on their personal journey of self-awareness and self-improvement.

Dedicated to Saraswati, who fires billions of neurons in my brain in trillions of ways, enabling my mind and body to serve

CONTENTS

INTRODUCTION: ALIGNING WITH MOON'S JOURNEY

Imagine standing beneath a star-studded sky, the moon's gentle glow casting a quiet brilliance over the earth. For millennia, this celestial dance of stars and planets has inspired wonder, guiding tides, seasons, and the intricate rhythms of life. Ancient sages, attuned to this interplay, observed the moon's journey—not merely as a scientific marvel but as a spiritual guide. Through their wisdom, the 27 *Nakshatras** *(refer Grey Pages - Glossary at the end for explanation of words with asterisk *)*, or lunar mansions, emerged as a profound map of cosmic and personal transformation.

The moon completes its orbit around the earth in roughly 27 days, pausing in each Nakshatra for approximately one day. These 27 segments of the moon's journey are not just astronomical markers; they embody distinct energies that reflect and influence our lives. From Ashwini's vitality and healing to Revati's peace and transcendence, the Nakshatras mirror the human journey—illuminating our struggles, desires, and growth with remarkable precision.

In "*Constellations Within: Stories and Practices from 27 Lunar Mansions to Empower You*" or simply "*Constellations Within*" —we embark on a transformative voyage through these lunar mansions. This book is not just a repository of celestial knowledge; it is a spiritual companion, guiding you to align with the cosmos to find clarity, balance, and renewal amidst the chaos of modern life.

Why This Journey Matters

In today's world, where we are pulled in countless directions, life often feels overwhelming. We pursue goals relentlessly, juggle responsibilities, and wrestle with fears, all while yearning for something deeper—peace, meaning, and connection. Yet these qualities remain elusive, obscured by the noise of daily demands.

The Nakshatras offer a timeless antidote. These celestial forces invite us to pause, reflect, and realign with life's natural rhythms. By consciously engaging with the energies of the Nakshatras, you can unlock pathways to:

- Self-Awareness: Recognize recurring patterns and discover their cosmic roots.
- Healing and Renewal: Release resistance and surrender to life's flow, restoring balance and vitality.
- Purpose and Direction: Navigate challenges with clarity, empowered by cosmic wisdom.

This journey isn't about mastering astrology as an abstract concept—it's about *living* astrology, weaving its timeless insights into your daily experiences for tangible transformation.

How This Book is Structured

Constellations Within is designed as a 27-day spiritual bootcamp, offering practical guidance to align with the Nakshatras' energies. Each chapter focuses on one lunar mansion and is divided into four parts:

1. **A Mythological Tale:** Stories serve as bridges between celestial truths and human understanding. The myth inspired *retelling* of each Nakshatra's story captures its essence, helping you connect deeply with its energy.
2. **Cosmic Message:** Each Nakshatra carries a universal lesson. There are materialistic connections and numerous worldly interpretations for each of the 27 which you may find in several texts. However there is a strong spiritual theme and associated cosmic message delivered by each Nakshatra and this book only focuses on such aspects for internal growth. These insights illuminate how its energy can guide you through life's challenges and aspirations.
3. **Practical Exercises:** Visualization, journaling, and mindfulness activities ground the Nakshatra's energy into your daily life, making its wisdom actionable and relatable.
4. **Advanced Practices:** For those seeking deeper engagement, these optional exercises provide further tools to harness the Nakshatra's transformative power.

By blending myth, insight, and action, this book invites you to move beyond reading and into an experiential journey of alignment.

In order to understand the concept of Nakshatras from a scientific perspective, you may scan the QR code below to see a 14 minute video. Alternatively one could jump to the 4 minute mark and watch for 4 minutes, until the 8 minute mark for the key message.

Scan QR code for a detailed explanation on Nakshatras

Video Courtesy : Vedic Astrology Through Animations

URL: https://www.youtube.com/watch?v=FA9C8YmMFlY

A Glimpse Into the Journey: Ashwini and Path of Renewal

Our journey through the book begins with Ashwini, the Nakshatra of healing and new beginnings. Through the story of Chyavana, a sage trapped in his own rigidity, we learn the profound lesson of surrender and trust. Chyavana's renewal wasn't achieved through struggle but through allowing himself to be guided by the healing energies of the Ashwini Kumaras.

This theme of renewal and release sets the tone for the journey ahead. Across the 27 lunar mansions, you will encounter lessons that are both universal and deeply personal, offering practical guidance to navigate modern challenges with grace.

Why Now?

The wisdom of the Nakshatras is more relevant today than ever before. In an era defined by uncertainty and rapid change, their timeless insights serve as anchors, grounding us amidst the turbulence. They provide a roadmap for clarity, balance, and resilience, reminding us that the answers we seek are often within ourselves—only reflected by mirrors of the stars.

Whether you're seeking clarity in relationships, healing from past wounds, or a deeper connection to the cosmos, this journey offers a way forward. By aligning with the Nakshatras' energies, you'll uncover profound truths about yourself and the universe, equipping you to navigate life with renewed purpose.

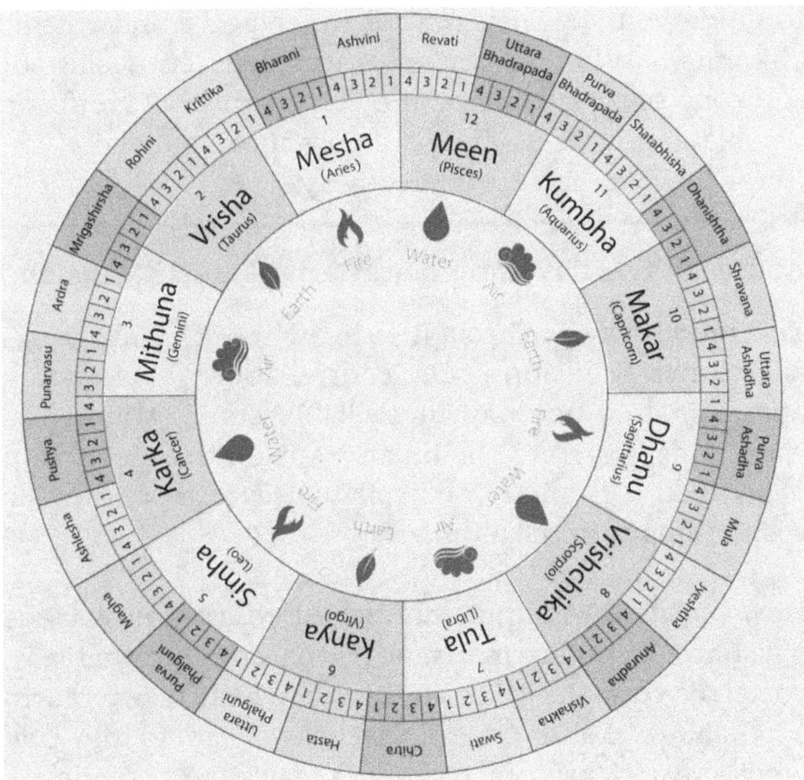

Image Source : Vedic Astrology Through Animations

HOW TO USE THIS BOOK

In today's fast-paced world, navigating through spiritual wisdom can feel daunting. *Constellations Within* is designed to be not just a book, but a transformative tool to guide your journey toward inner peace and cosmic alignment. Whether you're an astrology enthusiast or someone seeking balance and clarity, this book offers a flexible approach to fit seamlessly into your daily life. Here's how you can use it effectively:

Approach 1. Follow the Moon's Current Lunar Mansion

The moon travels through each of the 27 Nakshatras (aka lunar mansions, aka constellations), spending approximately one day in each. By starting with the chapter dedicated to the lunar mansion the moon is in *today*, you can align your spiritual exercises with the cosmic energy of the moment.

How to Begin: A simple online search can tell you the nakshatra or lunar mansion of the day. Alternatively, you may scan the QR code below, which takes you to a reliable website. On this webpage, go to the row which says 'Nakshatra' to know today's Lunar Mansion. For example, if the Nakshatra for today is mentioned as Ashwini, refer the *'Contents'* page of this book, and begin with the chapter, *Lunar Mansion 1: Ashwini.* There is a possibility of slight differences in spellings depending on the website, e.g. Lunar Mansion 19: 'Moola' might be spelt as 'Mool' or 'Mula', depending on where you search.

link to today's lunar mansion

The 27 lunar mansions are cyclical, meaning you can start your journey from any of them and proceed in a sequence thereafter.

Daily Practice: Spend one day with each chapter, immersing yourself in its theme, story, and exercises. Over 27 days, you'll complete the book and experience a full lunar cycle of transformation. If you are unable to do all the exercises, it is just fine. Find your rhythm, find what works for you and do at least one of them. Some of the exercises might appear repetitive. They will actually *feel different* if performed in the correct order with the suggested reflections. It is just fine even if they feel like repetition as they will serve their purpose to some extent. For the sounds which have been suggested, you may simply find an audio or video online using the same words which have been suggested.

Missed Days? No worries! Simply skip ahead to the current lunar mansion and continue. The book is designed to meet you where you are, amplifying your spiritual gains. However, consistency shall reward you with accelerated progress.

Approach 2. Read It Like a Novel

If structured timelines don't work for you, treat this book as a source of inspiration. Enjoy the rich mythological retellings, engaging analogies, and profound insights at your own pace.

> **Choose Your Path**: Read through the chapters sequentially or jump to the ones that resonate most with your current mood or challenges.
>
> **Selective Exercises**: Perform only the exercises that appeal to you or fit into your day. Even small actions shall create ripples of change in your life. Consistency is the key.

Approach 3. Focus on Weak or Afflicted Lunar Mansions

For those familiar with their birth chart, certain Nakshatras may stand out as weak or afflicted. These lunar mansions often represent areas of life where challenges arise and growth is needed.

> **Personalized Healing**: Identify your weak or afflicted Nakshatras and focus on the corresponding chapters. The practical and advanced exercises suggested in this book can help you pacify imbalances and harness their unique energies.
>
> **Lessons from the Stars**: These Nakshatras symbolize the spiritual lessons your soul has chosen to learn. By working with them consciously, you align with your cosmic purpose and accelerate your spiritual growth.

Why This Approach Works

Flexibility: The book accommodates all levels of spiritual practice, from daily rituals to occasional reflection.

Accessibility: No prior knowledge of astrology or astronomy is required. The insights and exercises are universally applicable, offering benefits to anyone willing to explore them.

Transformation: Whether you seek clarity, balance, or renewal, this book offers tools to navigate life's challenges with grace and purpose.

An Invitation to Align

The Nakshatras are more than celestial markers; they are spiritual allies—guides, teachers, and reflections of your deepest potential. As you move through these 27 days, approach each chapter with curiosity and openness. Allow the stories to resonate, the insights to inspire, and the exercises to ground you in the energies of each lunar mansion.

This is your journey—a journey of alignment, renewal, and empowerment. Over the next 27 days, you will reconnect with the natural rhythms of life, rediscover your inner peace, and unlock the cosmic energy within you.

Welcome to *Constellations Within*. The stars are calling. Shall we begin?

LUNAR MANSION 1: ASHWINI

The heavens whispered their secrets through the stars of **Aries**, their shimmering light ancient yet alive with meaning. At the forefront of this constellation stand **Sheratan (**Beta Arietis) and **Mesarthim (**Gamma Arietis), twin flames of cosmic guidance. Together, they form the astral gateway of **Ashwini Nakshatra**, where beginnings are not just moments in time but sparks of transformation.

Here, the symbol of the **Horse's Head**, governed by the enigmatic **Ketu**, takes the reins. It embodies a force that is both untamed and deeply intuitive, urging a leap of faith into the unknown. **Aries**, ruled by fiery **Mars**, infuses this celestial domain with the vigor of a warrior and the daring of a trailblazer. Yet, the true strength of Ashwini lies not in battle but in the quiet courage of healing and renewal.

The essence of this nakshatra is captured in a single, profound truth: **"Trust the inner force that guides bold beginnings. Action paired with surrender heals."**

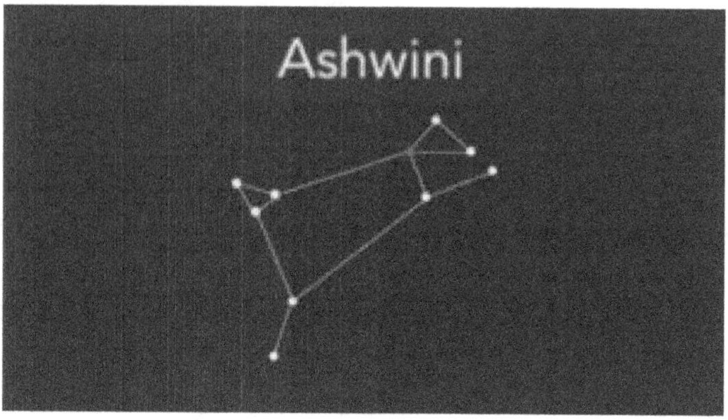

Image Source: https://popularvedicscience.com/astrology/ashwini-nakshatra

---

The Healing of *Chyavana**

Context for Readers

As per *Vedic Astrology** , (also known as ***Jyotisha***) the Nakshatras symbolize specific energies and life lessons. The first Nakshatra, Ashwini, is associated with vitality, healing, and new beginnings. The story of Chyavana, a sage who transforms from despair to renewed purpose through the intervention of the *Ashwini Kumaras** *(refer Grey Pages - Glossary at the end for explanation of words with asterisk *)* , celestial healers, highlights universal themes of surrender, trust, and action. This tale resonates with anyone navigating moments of stagnation, showing how renewal often lies in letting go of resistance and embracing change.

The Story

The forest breathed with a life of its own, a timeless dance of rustling leaves and whispering branches. Beneath the canopy of ancient banyan trees, Chyavana sat, still as stone. Once a sage of fiery brilliance, he was now veiled in shadows, his inner light dimmed by years of withdrawal. The moss crept up the rock where he perched, not out of malice but as if the forest sought to claim what no longer moved.

His back had hunched and bones had started turning brittle. He had believed that remaining still in meditation forever would liberate him. He had chosen this solitude to escape the illusions of the world, but what he found was not peace—it was stagnation. The still pond before him mirrored his decline. The man who stared back was a stranger: slumped, weary, his eyes dulled by endless searching that led nowhere.

One evening, the air shifted. The usual earthy stillness grew charged, the forest holding its breath. Birds fell silent, and the trees stood sentinel as if waiting for something extraordinary. And then, they came.

The Ashwini Kumaras, celestial twins of vitality and purpose, stepped into the clearing. Their presence was like the first rays of dawn after an endless night. One carried a flask glowing with a liquid that seemed alive; the other held a staff entwined with blooming vines. They moved as though the forest bent to their rhythm, their every step imbued with meaning.

Chyavana's voice cracked, a dry echo of defiance. "Who dares to intrude upon my retreat?"

The elder twin smiled, not with mockery but with quiet

conviction. "We do not intrude. We call."

"Call?" Chyavana's laugh was sharp, defensive. "I have turned from the world and its chaos. What could you offer me?"

The younger twin stepped forward, planting the staff in the ground. Vines unfurled, blooming in the space between them. "You misunderstand surrender, sage. Stillness is not freedom. It is fear, disguised."

The words struck like a drumbeat in the depths of Chyavana's being. His lips parted for a rebuttal, but none came. The forest around them seemed to hold its breath.

"Come," the elder twin urged, his tone neither commanding nor pleading. "A step forward is not the end of stillness but its beginning."

Though reluctance weighed heavily, Chyavana followed. They wove deeper into the forest, where light and shadow intertwined. At last, they reached a lake that seemed to hold the sun itself—a molten golden expanse, rippling with life.

"Enter," the elder twin said.

The sage hesitated, the air around the lake humming with possibility. "What lies within?" he whispered.

The younger twin smiled gently. "A truth you have forgotten. Step in, and you will see."

Chyavana's fingers curled into fists. For years, he had resisted movement, clung to the comfort of his stillness. Yet now, something stirred—a pull from within, faint yet undeniable. He stepped into the golden waters.

Warmth enveloped him, not just on his skin but in the very marrow of his being. The ripples carried memories: his youthful zeal, the paths he had chosen, the fears that had anchored him in place. The water did not erase these moments; it revealed them as threads in a pattern larger than his solitude.

When he emerged, the reflection in the lake startled him. His back was straight, his eyes clear, his body lighter—not transformed but renewed. The years of inertia fell away, leaving behind not a relic, but a man ready to act.

The twins stood waiting, their presence serene. "Healing is not found in retreat but in the courage to step forward," the elder twin said.

Before Chyavana could respond, the quiet of the forest was shattered by a cry. A young woman stumbled into the clearing, her face streaked with tears. "Please," she gasped. "My village is dying. Sickness consumes us, and I have nowhere to turn."

The twins exchanged a glance, with an unspoken understanding. They handed Chyavana the golden flask. "The waters healed you. Now let them flow outward."

Chyavana held the flask, its weight both literal and symbolic. For the first time in years, his heart stirred with purpose—not for himself, but for others. "Lead me to your people," he said to the woman, his voice steady.

She nodded, her steps quick as they disappeared into the embrace of the trees. Behind them, the twins' voices drifted like the wind itself.

"Action paired with surrender heals not just the self, but

the world."

And as the forest began to hum its eternal song once more, Chyavana felt the first true stirrings of life within him—not as a relic, but as a force in motion.

Moral of the Story

The story of Chyavana and the Ashwini Kumaras teaches that true healing begins when we trust the flow of life. Taking bold steps toward renewal, paired with surrender to what life offers, transforms despair into purpose. Whether in personal, professional, or emotional contexts, the path to healing lies not in avoiding struggle but in confronting it with courage and openness.

Modern-Day Relevance

In a world driven by control and perfectionism, many of us find ourselves trapped—whether in burnout, emotional stagnation, or the fear of failure. Chyavana's story reminds us that healing is not about regaining control but about surrendering to life's natural rhythms. For example:

> Professionally: Someone struggling with burnout may find renewal not by working harder but by stepping back and trusting their capacity to recover.
>
> Personally: A person grieving a loss might learn to embrace their emotions, finding healing not in avoidance but in acceptance.
>
> Leadership: Leaders facing challenges can discover that true strength lies in uplifting others through

their journey of renewal.

The Ashwini Kumaras teach us that healing is both an inner and outer journey. By trusting in the process and extending our renewal to others, we align with the flow of life, unlocking true vitality and purpose.

Real-Life Analogies for the New Seekers

1. Starting Over After Failure:

Imagine an entrepreneur whose business fails after years of effort. Overwhelmed by despair, they isolate themselves, convinced they can't succeed. One day, a mentor approaches with advice and encouragement, urging them to take a fresh step forward. By trusting the process and taking action —starting a new venture—they rediscover purpose and vitality, realizing that failure was a stepping stone, not an end.

Key Takeaway: Renewal comes when we let go of past disappointments, trust our abilities, and step into new opportunities.

2. Overcoming Emotional Burnout:

Picture a person overwhelmed by emotional burnout from caring for others, neglecting their own well-being. After hitting a breaking point, they join a support group that emphasizes self-care. Slowly, they learn to let go of guilt and embrace practices that nurture their own vitality, like mindfulness and rest. Replenished, they return to their caregiving roles with greater energy and balance.

Key Takeaway: Healing requires both action—taking care of oneself—and surrender—releasing guilt or resistance to change.

Practical Exercises for the Lunar Mansion

1. Visualization: The Healing Horse

Close your eyes and picture yourself riding a swift, radiant horse through an open field. The horse's energy is pure vitality, and with each gallop, it clears away doubts, fatigue, and fear. Feel the wind on your face and the steady rhythm of the ride, leaving you refreshed and inspired.

2. Journaling Prompt

Reflect on an area of your life where you feel stuck or stagnant.

> What is preventing you from moving forward?
>
> What first small step can you take toward renewal and healing?
>
> Describe a time when trust or surrender helped you through a challenge. How did it transform you?

3. Action for the Day

Begin a task or project you've been postponing, no matter how small. Whether it's organizing your desk or starting a creative venture, let the energy of beginnings propel you forward.

Advanced Exercises to Harness the Energy of Ashwini

a) Meditation with Sound

Purpose: Evoke Ashwini's swift and healing energy.

Meditate for 15 minutes to the sound of galloping horses. With each gallop, visualize yourself charging forward, breaking through barriers, and embracing vitality.

b) Connect to Nature

Purpose: Embody Ashwini's dynamic and energetic essence.

Take a morning run or brisk walk outdoors. Focus on the wind's touch and the rhythm of your breath. With every step, visualize yourself becoming lighter, freer, and more vibrant.

c) Perform a Service

Purpose: Channel Ashwini's healing energy into the world through you.

Help someone resolve an urgent issue. Whether it's delivering groceries to an elderly neighbor, sharing advice, or offering a quick solution to a colleague's problem, act swiftly and with care. Do not expect anything in return.

"Healing is not the absence of pain but the courage to begin again with trust in life's flow."

LUNAR MANSION 2: BHARANI

The universe often begins with a cry (or a big bang), raw and unfiltered, echoing through the cosmos like a heartbeat that refuses to fade. Beneath the fiery skies, the celestial dance of **35, 39, and 41 Arietis**, the fiery stars of Bharani Nakshatra, there lies a story of enduring strength and inevitable transformation—a tale whispered in the symbols of life itself.

Bharani, represented by the sacred ***Yoni****** (female reproductive organ), the vessel of creation, is ruled by **Venus**, the planet of life's pleasures and profound connections. Anchored in the zodiac sign of **Aries**, governed by the warrior energy of **Mars**, it vibrates with urgency—a push to move forward, to endure, to birth something new even in the face of life's most searing challenges.

Yet, Bharani's theme is not one of gentleness. Its lesson is that **life, in its rawest form, demands endurance.** It demands that you hold on through the contractions of existence, through the moments when the weight of the world presses hardest against your soul. To be born is an act of courage; to transform, an act of surrender.

The cosmic message of Bharani speaks to this duality: **"Endurance in challenges strengthens the soul. To feel**

reborn, embrace life fully, joys and sorrows alike."

It is here, beneath the stars of Bharani, that life's paradox unfolds. To transform is not to flee from pain, but to embrace it, letting its lessons guide you to a new self—a self reborn.

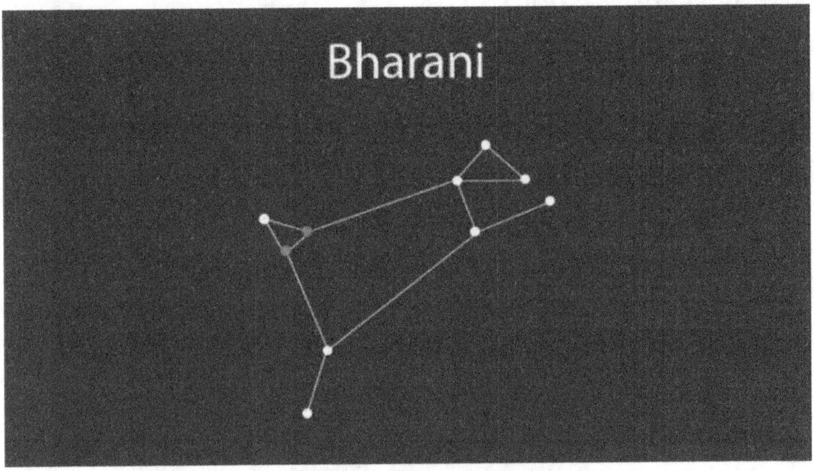

Image Source: https://popularvedicscience.com/astrology/bharani-nakshatra

---

The Story of *Yama*[*]: The Judge of Transformation

Context for Readers

In Indian mythology, Yama, the celestial lord of death, is not a harbinger of fear or doom but a compassionate guide and just arbiter. His role transcends the cessation of life, encompassing the delicate balance of the life-death-rebirth cycle. Yama ensures that each soul is fairly judged and guided according to their deeds, offering them the opportunity for spiritual growth.

This myth-inspired story of Yama as a mortal farmer named Arjuna highlights the transformative power of endurance. Through life's relentless challenges, Yama learns that struggle is not a curse but a crucible that refines the soul. This tale resonates universally, illustrating that adversity often serves as a path to inner strength and wisdom.

The Story

The fields stretched wide under an oppressive sun, their cracked earth whispering despair. Yet amidst the barrenness, a lone figure worked—Arjuna, a farmer, his back bent, his hands calloused. The drought had stolen the rivers, but not his resolve. He planted seeds in the desolate ground, his motions steady against the mockery of neighbors who had long abandoned their fields.

"You're a fool, Arjuna," they jeered. "The land is dead, and so is hope. Leave before it takes you too."

Arjuna straightened, brushing dust from his brow. "Life yields only to those who endure," he said simply, his voice weathered but unwavering. Then he turned back to his labor, a quiet defiance in each movement.

That night, under a sky void of stars, he knelt alone in his fields. The silence around him pressed heavy until it was broken by a voice, neither harsh nor gentle. "Why do you persist?"

Arjuna's head snapped up. Before him stood a woman cloaked in radiant light, her presence commanding yet serene. She was *Shakti*[*], the primordial force of creation and destruction.

"I persist because life demands it," Arjuna replied, his voice resolute despite his weariness. "Even in despair, life must hold meaning."

Shakti studied him, her eyes aglow with both challenge and approval. "Then prove it," she said, conjuring a small flame that danced above her palm, its light impossibly steady. "This is the Eternal Flame, the essence of life itself. Carry it to the summit of Mount Bharani, and you will discover the meaning you seek. But beware—the path will test you."

Arjuna reached for the flame, its warmth filling his hands and sparking a quiet determination in his heart. With no further words, he began his climb.

The mountain was unrelenting. Winds howled, tearing at him, the flame flickering dangerously in his grasp. Rains battered his body, soaking him to the bone. His muscles screamed in protest, and more than once, he stumbled, the flame quivering as though on the brink of extinction.

"What keeps me going?" Arjuna muttered as exhaustion clawed at him. Each step felt heavier than the last, and the temptation of heading back loomed like a shadow at his back. But each time his resolve faltered, the memory of his barren fields returned, tethering him to his purpose. The seeds he had planted, the land he refused to abandon —they reminded him that life was a promise kept, not a burden shrugged.

He cupped his hands around the flame, shielding it as though it were a fragile heartbeat. Blisters marred his skin, and his body ached from the climb, yet he pressed on.

At last, the summit emerged from the mist. Arjuna stood breathless, the Eternal Flame still alight in his hands. Shakti appeared once more, her radiance now softer, like a mother's pride.

"You have done well," she said. "But tell me, what have you learned?"

Arjuna gazed at the flame, his voice trembling as he spoke. "I have learned that life's flame is fragile yet unyielding. Its light does not come from ease but from struggle. Each trial makes it burn brighter. To carry it is not a burden—it is an honor."

Shakti smiled and touched his forehead. In that instant, Arjuna's mortal body fell away, and he stood as Yama, the celestial lord of death. The trials had forged him, granting him the wisdom to guide souls through life's ceaseless cycle of endings and beginnings.

As Yama descended Mount Bharani, the Eternal Flame no longer burned in his hands but within his being. Its light, steady and eternal, became his essence, illuminating his path as a guide through the cosmos.

Eons later, a weary soul, beaten down by life's trials, stood before Yama. "Why must we endure such pain?" the soul asked.

Yama knelt, his voice as steady as the flame that burned within him. "Because endurance transforms us. The fire of life shines not despite the winds and storms but because of them. Without struggle, we cannot grow. Without carrying the flame, we cannot know its light."

The soul gazed at Yama and saw the flickering flame within him—steady, unbroken, eternal. And in that moment, the soul understood: life's trials do not extinguish the flame; they are the reason it burns at all.

Moral of the Story

Transformation requires endurance. The trials we face in life are not meant to weaken us but to strengthen the light within. True growth comes when we embrace both the pain and the beauty of existence, knowing that every struggle adds to the brilliance of our flame.

Modern-Day Relevance

In today's fast-paced world, people often shy away from challenges, seeking comfort and instant solutions. Yet, Bharani's lesson is clear: life's most profound transformations come from enduring hardship.

> Professionally: Facing a difficult project , being in a demanding job or failing at a venture can feel overwhelming. Yama's journey teaches us to persevere, trusting that each trial is refining our skills and preparing us for greater responsibilities.
>
> Personally: Dealing with loss, heartbreak, or setbacks can be emotionally draining. Like Arjuna carrying the Eternal Flame, we must endure these trials to emerge stronger, with a deeper understanding of life's purpose.
>
> Spiritually: In moments of doubt or spiritual struggle, it's easy to feel lost. This story reminds us that growth requires endurance and that every

hardship carries the potential for transformation.

Yama's journey reminds us that endurance is the cornerstone of growth. Through life's storms, we do not lose our light—we learn to let it shine brighter.

Real-Life Analogies for the New Seekers

1: The Candle in the Wind: Imagine a person lighting a candle outdoors during a storm. The winds threaten to extinguish the flame at every moment. The person must shield it with their hands, steady their focus, and persevere despite the challenges. By the time the storm passes, the candle still burns, and the person realizes the effort was not just about preserving light—it was about their resilience and determination.

Key Takeaway:
Life's struggles are the winds, and the flame is your inner strength. Protecting and nurturing it makes you stronger, even as you face adversity.

2: The Marathon Runner: A runner preparing for a marathon doesn't stop training because the process is grueling. Each mile tests their resolve, pushing their body and mind to the limit. Yet, they continue, knowing the journey is more about personal growth than the finish line. By enduring the pain and exhaustion, they discover their true potential.

Key Takeaway:
Just as the runner endures the journey for the sake of growth, life's challenges are opportunities to

build strength, resilience, and wisdom.

The tale of Bharani encourages us to embrace life's trials as opportunities for growth, just as a flame burns brighter when tested by the elements. For new seekers, this is a powerful reminder that challenges are not barriers but stepping stones on the path to enlightenment.

Practical Exercise for the Lunar Mansion

1. Visualization: The Bridge of Endurance

Close your eyes and imagine yourself standing before a vast, rushing river. A narrow, sturdy bridge stretches across, symbolizing a challenging phase of your life. As you walk across, feel the weight of your burdens lightening with each step. When you reach the other side, visualize yourself stronger, grounded, and filled with inner peace.

2. Journaling Prompt

Reflect on a time when you endured a difficult situation.

What did you learn about yourself through this experience?

How did it change or strengthen you?

Write about an area of your life where you feel tested right now. What small steps can you take to face these challenges with courage and resilience?

3. Action for the Day

Consciously take on a small, challenging task. Whether it's completing a difficult work assignment or addressing an uncomfortable conversation, approach it with patience and determination, knowing that every effort builds inner strength.

Advanced Exercises to Harness the Energy of Bharani

a) Meditation with Sound

Purpose: Align with Bharani's transformative energy.

Meditate for 15 minutes to the resonant beats of tribal drums. Feel the rhythm grounding you, instilling endurance, and connecting you to your primal strength.

b) Connect to Nature

Purpose: Experience Bharani's grounding and transformative essence.

Spend time near water, such as a river, stream or ocean. Observe its steady movement, symbolizing life's constant flow and resilience. Allow its presence to remind you of your own strength to navigate challenges.

c) Perform a Service

Purpose: Embrace Bharani's theme of endurance through compassionate action.

Support someone enduring a difficult time. Whether it's offering encouragement, lending an ear, or helping them manage their workload, your act of kindness mirrors Bharani's lesson of enduring together. Do not expect anything in return.

"True transformation is born in the crucible of endurance, where one learns to embrace both joy and pain."

LUNAR MANSION 3: KRITTIKA

Under the velvet canopy of night, six stars blazed like embers in the heavens—the celestial fire of **Krittika**, the sharp-edged lunar mansion. Known to astronomers as part of the Pleiades, the "Seven Sisters" or "M45," this cluster was revered in ancient skies not for its number but for its meaning. To the seers, these six stars symbolized precision and power, their fiery light cutting through darkness with clarity and purpose.

Ruled by the **Sun** and residing across the zodiac signs of **Aries** and **Taurus**, Krittika embodied dual forces: the bold ignition of **Mars'** energy and the grounded discernment of **Venus**. Its symbol, the **spear** or **knife**, reflected its essence—tools not of destruction, but of transformation. In the cosmic dance, Krittika's fire was not wild or reckless; it was a cleansing force, severing illusions to reveal the unvarnished truth beneath.

The theme of Krittika spoke directly to the soul's journey: **"True power lies in cutting away illusions. Clarity emerges through courage and precision."** Its celestial light whispered this wisdom, guiding those bold enough to wield the tools of discernment, to embrace the courage it takes to strip away the unnecessary, and to step forward into a life defined by truth.

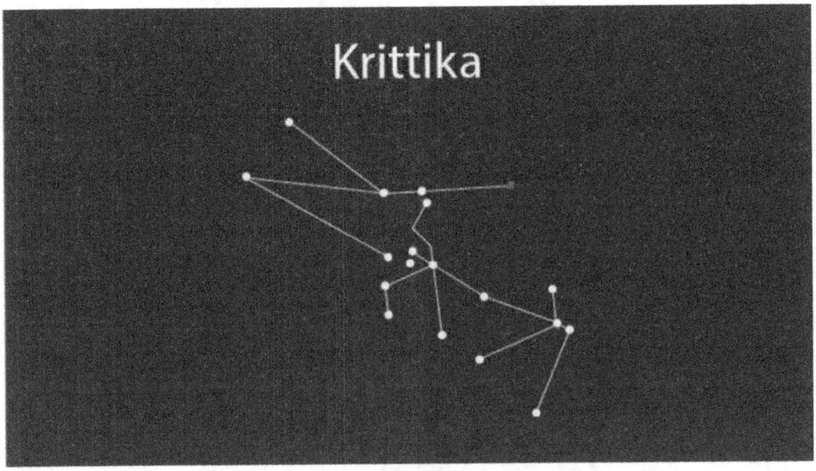

Image Source: https://popularvedicscience.com/astrology/krittika-nakshatra

---

The Tale of *Kartikeya and the Demon of Deception**

Context for Readers

In Indian mythology, the battle between gods and demons often represents deeper struggles—between truth and illusion, light and darkness, clarity and confusion. These stories are not merely about physical battles; they symbolize the eternal quest for self-awareness and the triumph of inner virtues over external challenges.

Kartikeya, also known as Skanda or Murugan, is a revered deity in Indian mythology. He is the warrior son of *Shiva**, the destroyer god, and Parvati, the goddess of power. Known for his sharp intellect, valor, and spiritual wisdom, Kartikeya embodies the ability to overcome challenges with precision and insight.

This myth-inspired tale of Kartikeya and the Demon of Deception revolves around his confrontation with *Tarakasura*[*], a demon whose strength lay not in brute force but in his mastery of illusion. Tarakasura's power to manipulate reality represents the deceptions and falsehoods we often face in life, while Kartikeya's triumph reflects the clarity and discernment needed to see through illusions and uncover the truth. This story resonates with universal themes of perception, courage, and self-mastery, transcending cultural boundaries.

The six stars of the Krittika Nakshatra represent the six Krittikas (celestial nymphs) who raised Kartikeya. After his birth, Kartikeya was nurtured by these six divine mothers, symbolizing the nurturing and fiery qualities of the Krittika Nakshatra. It is known for its fiery energy, sharpness, and the ability to cut away impurities and illusions, much like Kartikeya's role in defeating demons and restoring cosmic balance.

The Story

In the golden age of gods and demons, the shadow of Tarakasura grew like a storm over the realms. The demon, blessed by powerful boons, wielded not only strength but also a sinister mastery over illusions. His deceptions were so intricate that they turned allies into enemies and made the gods question even their own senses. His rule was chaos—one built on fear and the shattering of clarity.

The gods, weary of his growing dominance, turned to Kartikeya, the warrior son of Shiva and Parvati. Known for his unerring precision and courage, Kartikeya was the only hope to confront a foe who thrived in shadows.

*Indra**, the king of the gods, approached him with urgency.

"You must confront Tarakasura," Indra implored, his voice shaky with concern. "But know this—his strength is not in his might but in his illusions. To defeat him, you must see what others cannot."

Kartikeya, resolute yet cautious, prepared himself for the task. Armed with his celestial spear, Vel, he journeyed to the heart of Tarakasura's domain—a battlefield veiled in thick smoke and shimmering mirages. Here, nothing was as it seemed; the ground itself felt like a shifting tide.

When Kartikeya arrived, the demon materialized, his form grotesque and towering, his laughter rippling through the haze. "So, the gods send a child to fight me?" Tarakasura sneered. "Do you not know? I cannot be touched. I am everywhere and nowhere."

Kartikeya raised his spear, his stance firm. But as he lunged, Tarakasura's form shattered into countless replicas, each identical and each mocking. "Strike me if you can!" the illusions taunted in unison.

For days, Kartikeya fought. His spear cut through form after form, but each dissolved into smoke. His muscles burned, his breaths grew ragged, and still the battlefield swirled with falsehoods. Exhausted, he paused, his spear heavy in his hands.

Then, he sat down.

In the midst of chaos, Kartikeya stilled himself. The illusions clamored around him, their voices rising in waves, but he let them wash over him. His mind, sharp and disciplined, began to seek not the noise but the silence beneath it. He closed his eyes and listened—not to the laughter, but to the faint rhythm that thrummed beneath the battlefield.

There it was. A tremor in the earth, a heartbeat separate from the noises made by the illusions. A truth that could not be concealed. He opened his eyes, and the world shifted. The illusions shattered like fragile glass, leaving the battlefield stark and bare.

In the shadows, Tarakasura's true form slouched—a small, desperate figure, no longer grand or terrifying, but pitiful in its attempts to hide. Kartikeya rose, his movements deliberate, and hurled his spear with unwavering precision. Vel struck true, piercing the demon's heart.

Tarakasura's scream tore through the air, not with rage but with release. The swirling illusions dissipated, leaving the world clear and steady once more. Kartikeya approached the fallen demon, his grip on his spear firm, expecting defiance. But Tarakasura's voice, now trembling, carried only sorrow.

"You have freed me," Tarakasura whispered, his form beginning to dissolve into golden light. "I was cursed to create illusions, to live trapped in the falsehoods that even I despised. Your clarity… your courage… has broken the curse."

The light grew brighter, enveloping the battlefield, until

Tarakasura's essence vanished entirely, leaving no trace of the demon who once sowed chaos. Kartikeya stood in stillness, his heart filled with understanding. The battle had not been one of destruction but of precision and truth. He had cut through not just the illusions of the enemy but the doubts within himself.

As he turned to leave, the forest around him whispered its wisdom, a truth as timeless as the stars: "True power lies in cutting away illusions. Clarity emerges through courage and precision."

Moral of the Story

Kartikeya's triumph over Tarakasura shows us that the greatest battles are not external but within. The tools for victory—discernment, clarity, and courage—are accessible to us all.

True power lies not in brute strength but in discernment. To overcome challenges, one must see beyond the illusions of fear, ego, and deception. Clarity emerges when we quiet the noise around us and trust in the truth within.

Modern-Day Relevance

In today's fast-paced world, we are surrounded by illusions—social media facades, misinformation, and the pressure to conform to societal expectations. Kartikeya's story reminds us to cultivate discernment and clarity.

> Professionally: In a competitive workplace, the ability to discern meaningful opportunities from distractions ensures success. Kartikeya's lesson reminds us to focus on precision rather than

spreading ourselves thin.

Personally: In relationships, misunderstandings often arise from illusions or assumptions. Taking time to reflect and seek clarity, as well as to see beyond the surface strengthens bonds, just as Kartikeya's stillness revealed the truth.

Spiritually: Meditation and mindfulness practices are modern tools to quiet the mind, much like Kartikeya sitting amidst chaos. These practices allow us to cut through internal illusions and align with our true selves.

Krittika's energy teaches us the courage to cut through illusions and the precision to act with purpose, lighting the path to wisdom and truth.

Real-Life Analogies for the New Seekers

1. The Foggy Windshield

Imagine driving on a foggy morning with your windshield blurred. No matter how skilled you are as a driver, navigating the road becomes almost impossible without clearing the fog. When you wipe the windshield, the path ahead becomes clear, and you can proceed with confidence.

Lesson: Life's illusions—doubts, fears, and distractions—act like the fog. Without discernment and clarity (wiping the fog), you cannot see the truth or make precise decisions. Like Kartikeya, you must pause, focus inward, and clear your mind to see reality as it is.

2. Sorting Through Fake News

In today's digital age, we are often bombarded with conflicting information. Distinguishing between truth and deception can feel overwhelming, much like Kartikeya facing the illusions of Tarakasura. When you pause to fact-check and analyze, the "illusions" of misinformation dissolve, revealing the truth.

Lesson: Precision and discernment, much like Kartikeya's pause on the battlefield, allow you to cut through the noise and focus on what truly matters. Clarity is not about rushing to act but about taking the time to perceive correctly.

Clarity is achieved not through brute force but by calming the mind and seeing beyond the surface. The illusions of life—fear, deception, and distractions—can only be overcome with courage and focus. True power lies in stillness and discernment, not in reacting impulsively.

Practical Exercises for the Lunar Mansion

1. Visualization: The Blade of Clarity

Close your eyes and imagine holding a gleaming blade, forged in the fires of courage. Picture yourself using this blade to cut through dense fog, symbolizing confusion, doubt, or illusions in your life. As the fog clears, a path of clarity and purpose emerges before you. Feel the empowerment of discernment guiding your steps.

2. Journaling Prompt

Reflect on a situation where you had to make a tough decision to move forward.

What did you gain from choosing clarity over comfort?

How can this experience guide you in your current challenges?

Write about areas of your life where illusions or attachments cloud your judgment. What steps can you take to confront them?

3. Action for the Day

Choose one task or habit that no longer serves your highest purpose and let it go. This could be decluttering a space, unfollowing distractions on social media, or addressing a lingering conflict with honesty.

Advanced Exercises to Harness the Energy of Krittika

a) Meditation with Sound

Purpose: Channel Krittika's sharp and discerning energy.

Meditate for 15 minutes to the crackling of a campfire with subtle creaking wood. Imagine the flames cutting through illusions, bringing clarity and courage.

b) Connect to Nature

Purpose: Embody Krittika's cutting and transformative essence.

Spend time near a bonfire or under the sun. Reflect on the transformative power of fire and light, which burn away what no longer serves to reveal clarity and truth.

c) Perform a Service

Purpose: Use Krittika's discerning energy to uplift others.

Help someone gain clarity in their life. This could mean offering honest advice, helping them organize their thoughts, or guiding them in making a clear decision. Do not expect anything in return.

"Clarity is a blade that cuts through illusion, but it takes courage to wield it against our deepest fears."

LUNAR MANSION 4: ROHINI

Under the golden glow of **Aldebaran** (Alpha Tauri), the brilliant star of **Rohini**, the cosmos seemed to breathe with life itself. Anchored in the heart of **Taurus**, this lunar mansion shimmered with the promise of **abundance** and **creation**. To the ancient seers, Rohini was the celestial **chariot**, drawn by the **Moon's** nurturing hand, carrying the **fertile** energy of existence forward in an unending flow.

Rohini's zodiac, ruled by **Venus**, radiated beauty, love, and the fertile potential of the earth. Its light was not harsh or fleeting; it was steady and luminous, a reflection of nature's gentle yet unstoppable force to create, renew, and thrive. Beneath this mansion, the mundane transformed into the extraordinary: the seed became the tree, the idea became the masterpiece, and life unfolded in its most vibrant forms.

The spiritual message of Rohini whispered an eternal truth: **"Celebrate life's creative flow; to exist is to thrive."** Its celestial light reminded all who gazed upon it that creation is not just an act—it is a state of being. In the rhythm of existence itself lies the power to flourish, to nurture, and to rejoice in the boundless beauty of life.

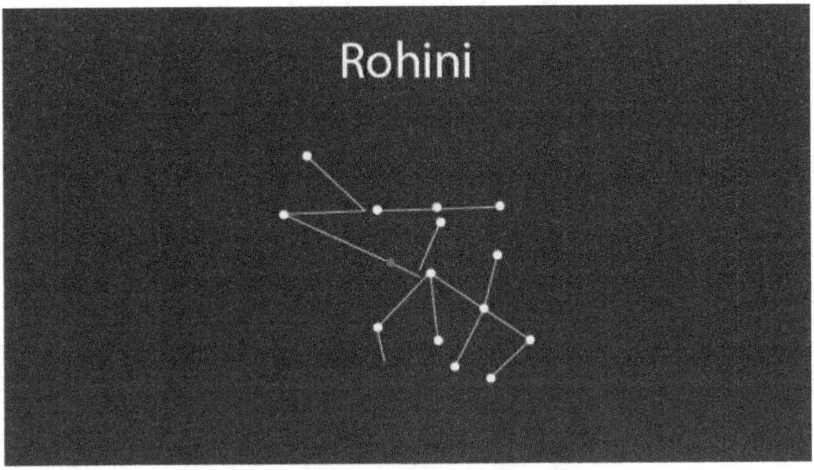

Image Source: https://popularvedicscience.com/astrology/rohini-nakshatra

---

The Tale of *Soma*[*] and Rohini

Context for Readers

In Indian mythology, the Moon (Soma) is more than a celestial body; it is a nurturer, a source of life and rhythm. The Moon interacts with 27 Nakshatras, or lunar mansions, or constellations along its celestial path, each imbued with unique energies and lessons. The fourth Nakshatra, Rohini, symbolizes abundance and creation, celebrated for her vibrancy and the life-giving energy she represents.

This myth-inspired tale of Soma and Rohini reflects the universal struggle between indulgence and responsibility, love and duty. It reveals the delicate balance needed to sustain harmony in relationships and nature. This story transcends cultural boundaries, offering timeless wisdom on creating and sharing abundance while maintaining balance.

The Story

In the vast expanse of the heavens, Soma, the Moon god, moved gracefully across the sky, his silvery glow nourishing life on the earth below. Yet his heart belonged to Rohini, the most radiant amongst his 27 wives (the 27 Nakshatras). Rohini's energy was pure vitality—a ceaseless flow of creation. Wherever her light touched, life awakened: rivers surged, blossoms unfurled, and seeds stirred within the Earth, yearning to grow.

Soma always found himself lingering in Rohini's presence, drawn to the vibrancy she exuded. While the other Nakshatras twinkled in quiet constancy, Rohini danced. Her movements were an ode to existence itself, each step a celebration of abundance. Soma's visits to her became more frequent, and though his path should have been shared equally among all the Nakshatras, his heart betrayed him and them.

The gods began to murmur. "Soma disrupts the harmony of creation," they said. The balance of the cosmos faltered as the other Nakshatras dimmed in neglect. Indra, king of the gods, confronted Soma. "Creation thrives on balance," Indra reminded him. "Without rhythm, life cannot endure."

Though Soma nodded in agreement, his heart rebelled. How could he turn away from Rohini's brilliance? She was life itself, irresistible and infinite. His defiance continued, and so did the imbalance.

One day, the sage-king *Daksha**, father to the Nakshatras, could no longer bear it. After all, 26 of his 27 daughters were suffering. His voice thundered through the heavens, his fury shaking the constellations. "Soma, your favoritism dishonors my daughters and weakens their divine purpose. You disrupt the cycles of life itself!" In his wrath, Daksha cursed Soma: "Your brilliance shall wane! Your light will diminish, and with it, the vitality you bring to creation shall be gone."

As the curse took hold, Soma's radiance began to fade. The once-thriving rivers slowed to a trickle, crops withered under a pale, sickly moonlight, and a stillness blanketed the Earth. The Nakshatras wept, their luminous harmony fractured. Rohini, however, refused to succumb to despair. "If Soma's light fades, then I shall restore it," she vowed, her voice steady with resolve.

Rohini descended to Earth, her steps gentle as dew yet potent with life. Where she walked, barren fields sprouted green shoots, and dry riverbeds began to stir. She moved through lifeless landscapes, her dance coaxing the hidden vitality from the Earth. Yet, despite her efforts, the glow of creation remained faint. The Moon's waning light was too weak to sustain life.

Desperate, Rohini ascended to her father Daksha's celestial court. "Your curse punishes not just Soma but all of creation," she implored. "Restore him, and I promise to safeguard the balance you cherish."

Daksha's expression was as unyielding as stone. "Balance is not begged for, child. It is created. Let Soma and the cosmos earn their renewal."

Rohini returned to Earth, determined to awaken a force greater than her own. Her dance became a hymn not only to life but to Soma's indomitable spirit. Her movements were no longer solitary—they were a call to unity. The other 26 Nakshatras, moved by her devotion, joined her, their combined lights weaving patterns of renewal across the heavens.

As their celestial harmony unfolded, even the barren Earth began to hum with vitality. Rivers surged anew, crops thrived, and the stars above pulsed in rhythm with their dance. The skies, now alight with this collective brilliance, caught the attention of Brahma, the Creator. "Rohini has shown that creation is not bound by curses but thrives through celebration and unity," Brahma declared. "Let Soma's light return, not as it was, but with a rhythm that honors all."

With a wave of his hand, Soma's brilliance was restored. Yet it now waxed and waned, and moved around in a cycle that ensured each of the 27 Nakshatras shared equally in his presence. Harmony was reborn, and life flourished once more.

As Soma's radiance returned, he turned to Rohini. Her light had grown softer, her once-vivid hues now subdued. "You gave a part of your essence to restore mine?" Soma enquired, his voice filled with gratitude.

Rohini's smile was serene, her glow steady. "True abundance is not in possessing but in creating. To thrive is to share, to celebrate life's infinite flow."

From that day, the celestial bond between Soma and

Rohini became eternal. The Moon's waxing and waning became a reminder of the cycles of life: beginnings and endings, growth and renewal. And in the night sky, Rohini shines bright, a testament to the truth that life's creative flow is not bound by limitations but thrives when shared.

Moral of the Story

Abundance and creation are sustained by balance, not excess. Passion and love thrive when shared responsibly, ensuring harmony in relationships and life. Soma's waxing and waning remind us that growth and creation are cyclical—true fulfillment comes when we create and share without attachment or favoritism.

Modern-Day Relevance

In today's world, people often equate abundance with material wealth and personal gain. Rohini's story teaches us that true abundance lies in what we create together and how we share it.

> Professional Scenario: A manager focusing solely on their favorite project may neglect team dynamics, leading to imbalance and burnout. Soma's story reminds us to distribute attention wisely, ensuring all areas thrive together.
>
> Lesson: Success stems from balancing passion with responsibility.
>
> Personal Scenario: A person deeply invested in one relationship may unintentionally neglect others, leading to disharmony. Rohini's energy teaches us

that love grows when shared equitably.

Lesson: Celebrate the beauty of connections without exclusivity to foster abundance in all relationships.

Spiritually: We can cultivate gratitude and abundance by aligning with life's rhythms and giving freely of our time, energy, or resources to uplift others.

Rohini's energy reminds us to celebrate life's creative flow, not as isolated beings but as part of a vibrant, interconnected whole. To exist is to thrive, and to thrive is to create

---

Real-Life Analogies for the New Seekers

1. The Overworked Artist

Imagine an artist who pours all their energy into creating one masterpiece while neglecting other responsibilities. Their work might shine temporarily, but their relationships, health, and broader commitments begin to suffer. To thrive, they must balance their creative passion with the needs of their life, much like Soma had to share his presence among the Nakshatras.

Key Takeaway: True creativity and abundance flourish when balanced with discipline and responsibility.

2. A Gardener's Balance

Picture a gardener who waters only one plant in their garden because it blooms beautifully, neglecting the others. Over time, the garden becomes uneven, with some plants thriving while others wither. When the gardener learns to distribute care evenly, the entire garden flourishes, creating harmony and abundance.

Key Takeaway: Abundance is not just about focusing on what's most appealing but nurturing all aspects of life for sustainable growth.

Practical Exercises for the Lunar Mansion

1. Visualization: The Garden of Creation

Close your eyes and imagine a lush, vibrant garden, symbolizing the abundance and creativity within you. Visualize yourself planting seeds in fertile soil, each seed representing a dream or idea. See the plants sprouting and blossoming, filling the air with their fragrance. Feel the joy and fulfillment of nurturing life's creative flow.

2. Journaling Prompt

Reflect on areas of your life where you experience abundance.

> What brings you the greatest sense of fulfillment and joy?
>
> How can you cultivate more of this energy in your daily life?

Write about a creative idea or passion project you've been nurturing. How can you take the next step to help it grow?

3. Action for the Day

Engage in a creative activity that brings you joy. Whether it's cooking a special meal, painting, gardening, or writing, let yourself immerse in the process and celebrate the act of creation.

Advanced Exercises to Harness the Energy of Rohini

a) Meditation with Sound

Purpose: Align with Rohini's abundant and creative energy.

Meditate for 15 minutes to melodic flute harmonized with birdsong. Visualize a garden blooming within you, symbolizing creativity and abundance.

b) Connect to Nature

Purpose: Embrace Rohini's fertile and nurturing essence.

Spend time in a garden, park, or natural space. Observe the plants and flowers around you, noting how they grow effortlessly in harmony with nature. Use this as inspiration for your own creative pursuits.

c) Perform a Service

Purpose: Share Rohini's nurturing energy with others.

Plant something—whether it's a tree, a flower, or herbs—in your community or gift a plant to someone. Your act of nurturing symbolizes the cycle of creation and abundance. Do not expect anything in return.

"To create is to align with abundance; life thrives in the joy of its own existence."

LUNAR MANSION 5: MRIGASHIRA

In the velvety expanse of the night sky, **Lambda Orionis (Meissa)** and **Phi Orionis**, the guiding stars of Mrigashira, shimmered like a beacon for wanderers. These celestial markers, embodying the spirit of the **Deer's Head**, whispered of restless curiosity, an eternal quest written in the fabric of the cosmos. Governed by **Mars**, the energy here was bold and piercing, yet yearning—forever chasing a truth that seemed just out of reach.

Beneath this stellar canopy, the earth stirred with the pulse of its own seekers. Among them, the faint, timeless hum of **Taurus and Gemini** wove through the heavens, their ruling deities, **Venus and Mercury**, lending voices to the desires of the heart and the whispers of the mind. This was a mansion of paradox—where the earthy comfort of **Taurus** met the cerebral curiosity of **Gemini**, and where the dance between what we want and what we seek unfolded.

The spiritual theme of **Mrigashira** was clear: a **Quest for Meaning**, yet its true challenge lay in the insight hidden beneath its stars: **"Seek beyond the material. True meaning arises from the awareness of your inner self."**

Against this celestial backdrop, our story begins—a tale of restlessness, revelations, and a search that would traverse the boundaries of the seen and the unseen.

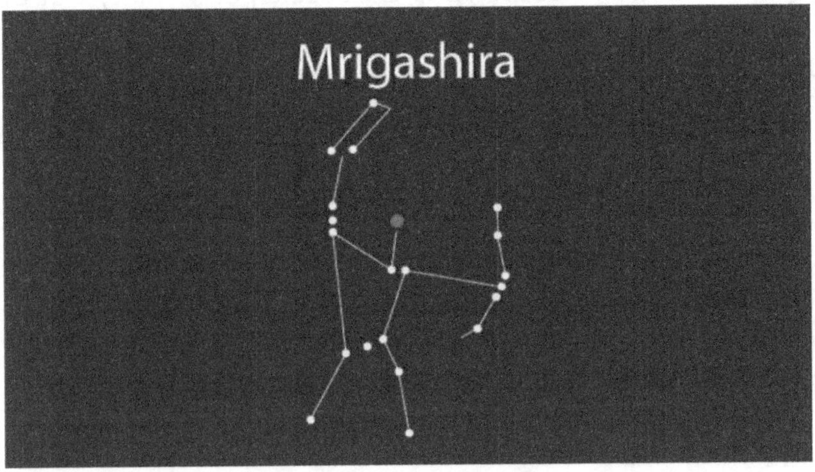

Image Source: https://popularvedicscience.com/astrology/Mrigashira-nakshatra

The Tale of *Rudra and the Elusive Deer**

Context for Readers

Indian mythology is deeply rooted in stories that explore the human experience through divine characters and cosmic principles. Among these tales, the figure of Rudra, a fierce and solitary form of the god Shiva, represents transformation, destruction of ignorance, and the pursuit of deeper truths.

The concept of *maya**, or illusion, is central to Indian philosophy. Maya is the veil that distorts reality, trapping beings in cycles of desire and suffering. The search for meaning often involves navigating and transcending maya to uncover inner truths.

This myth-inspired story of Rudra and the Elusive Deer, symbolizes the universal quest for meaning. The deer, known as the *Mriga**, represents the ultimate truth or

self-realization—something that feels perpetually out of reach. Rudra's journey through celestial forests and his eventual transformation mirrors the struggles we all face in searching for fulfillment. The story is not just about gods and mystical creatures; it's a reflection of our own restless hearts and the answers we find within.
Through this tale, the reader is invited to explore the idea that true meaning is not something external to be captured but an internal realization to be embraced. It's a story that transcends culture, resonating with anyone who has ever searched for purpose amidst the illusions of life.

The Story

In the eternal expanse of the intergalactic celestial forest, a mysterious deer wandered—its coat shimmering with the hues of dawn, its eyes holding the depth of infinite skies. The divine Mriga, a being of maya (illusion), was said to embody the essence of truth. Yet it was known to elude all who sought it, slipping between realms like whispers of the wind.

Far across the heavens, Rudra, the embodiment of the storm within Lord Shiva, paced with unrest. A god of unmatched power, his presence could command both creation and destruction, yet an invisible restlessness bore down on him. The battles he had waged, the austerities endured—they felt like fragments of an incomplete melody. "What am I missing?" he murmured, the words rising like smoke from a fire too long untended.

One day, a celestial sage crossed his path, sensing the turbulence within him. "You seek the Mriga," the sage said, his voice like the rustle of leaves. "But know this—the journey will demand more than strength or will. Are you prepared to be tested?"

Rudra's eyes flashed with determination. He needed answers, and he would not turn away.

The journey spanned realms painted by cosmic extremes—asteroid fields of fire that blazed with unspoken truths, mountains of ice that froze thoughts mid-breath. At last, Rudra entered the sacred forest where the Mriga was said to roam. The air here was different, heavy with a silence that seemed to listen as much as it stilled.

Then, like a fleeting sunrise, the Mriga appeared.

Its form was otherworldly, its movements liquid grace. Rudra's breath caught, his focus sharpening to a single point. The deer stood poised for an instant, its eyes meeting his, before leaping into the depths of the forest. Without hesitation, Rudra pursued.

Through streams and shadows, across cliffs and glaciers, the chase continued. The Mriga was always just beyond reach, its presence a tantalizing promise, its steps whispering of answers yet unseen. Days folded into nights, and Rudra's pursuit grew fevered. His strength faltered, but his pride refused to yield.

"Why do you flee?" he shouted one day, his voice raw, reverberating against the ancient trees. For the briefest moment, the Mriga turned, its gaze meeting his. It held no malice, only an enigmatic stillness that rooted Rudra in place. Before he could decipher its meaning, the deer vanished once more.

At last, exhaustion claimed him. Beneath the wide embrace of a banyan tree, Rudra collapsed. His body ached, his mind spun, and the forest—once vivid with purpose—now blurred into an unrelenting quiet.

"What is the point?" he muttered, staring at his calloused hands and blistered body, as he lay flat on the bare ground without an ounce of energy left. The air around him seemed to echo his question, but instead of answering, it replayed his steps: the thunder of his pursuit, the crackling leaves underfoot, the breathless urgency in his chest.

Gradually, the storm within him began to settle. As his mind quieted, the forest's rhythm came alive—the rustling leaves, the distant hum of a stream, the soft pulse of his own heartbeat. The chase replayed itself in his memory, not as a failure but as a reflection.

"The deer was never the goal," Rudra realized, his voice barely more than a whisper. "It mirrored my own longing. The journey was not about reaching it, but about understanding what was driving me."

In the stillness of his surrender, the Mriga appeared once more. Its steps were slow, deliberate, and this time, Rudra did not rise to pursue. He met its gaze with calm clarity, his heart no longer racing. The deer approached, its coat aglow, and bowed its head.

"You have found what you sought," came a voice, resonant yet without source. "True meaning does not lie in pursuit or in the catch. It is discovered in stillness. You are the seeker, but you are also the answer."

The Mriga dissolved into a cascade of golden light, flowing into Rudra's very being. Where once there was restlessness, there was now a quiet knowing—a wholeness that neither strength nor conquest had ever brought him.

As Rudra rose, he noticed the forest anew. His energy replenished. The same trees, the same streams—but they shimmered with a beauty he had never seen before. The vibrant blossoms, the sparkling rivers, the harmony in the air—it was not the forest that had changed but his own perception.

The chase had not transformed the world; it had transformed him.

Moral of the Story

True meaning is not something external to be chased or captured. It is realized within, through self-awareness and stillness. The search for meaning often reflects our inner state, and when we quiet the storm within, we find that the answers have always been with us.

Modern-Day Relevance

In today's world, many of us are like Rudra, chasing external validations—success, possessions, or recognition—believing they hold the key to fulfillment. Mrigashira's lesson reminds us that:

> Professionally: Purpose isn't found in titles or accolades but in the impact and authenticity of one's work.

Personally: Meaningful relationships are not about control or possession but about understanding and presence.

Spiritually: Fulfillment comes not from external achievements but from inner clarity and self-awareness.

The story of Rudra and the Mriga calls us to pause, reflect, and realize that the answers we seek are not "out there." They reside within, waiting for us to awaken.

Real-Life Analogies for the New Seekers

1. The Career Ladder Chase:

Imagine a professional tirelessly chasing promotions and accolades, believing they will bring happiness and fulfillment. Despite achieving milestones, an emptiness lingers.

Lesson: Like Rudra chasing the deer, the professional may realize that external achievements can't fill an internal void. Fulfillment comes from understanding their true values and aligning their work with a deeper purpose.

2. The Social Media Obsession:

Think of someone constantly seeking validation through likes, shares, and comments. They strive to present the perfect image, hoping it will make them feel whole.

Lesson: Just as Rudra discovered the deer was

a reflection of his own restlessness, this person may realize that inner peace and self-worth can't be captured externally. True meaning comes from self-acceptance and living authentically.

Rudra's journey teaches us that our search for meaning isn't a destination but a process of self-awareness. The answers we seek are not external treasures but reflections of the truths within us. When we stop chasing illusions and look inward, we realize we already hold the key to our fulfillment.

Practical Exercise for the Lunar Mansion

1. Visualization: The Lantern of Meaning

Close your eyes and imagine yourself walking through a dark forest, holding a glowing lantern. The lantern's light represents your inner wisdom, guiding you through the shadows of uncertainty. As you walk, the light reveals a treasure—an answer or realization that brings clarity and meaning to something that you are struggling with in your life at this point. This need not be an actual solution, but imagine the treasure bringing you the joy that you would have felt had you found the solution.

2. Journaling Prompt

Reflect on a question or dilemma you have been grappling with recently.

What are you truly seeking in this situation?

How can you trust your intuition to guide you toward an answer?

Write about a time when searching for answers led you to unexpected insights. How did that experience shape you?

3. Action for the Day

Dedicate some time to explore a topic or activity that intrigues you, whether it's reading about a philosophical question, journaling about your goals, or spending quiet time contemplating life's mysteries. Let your curiosity guide you.

Advanced Exercises to Harness the Energy of Mrigashira

a) Meditation with Sound

Purpose: Align with Mrigashira's questing and reflective energy.

Meditate for 15 minutes to the sound of gentle wind chimes. Let the delicate tones guide you on an inner quest for meaning and self-discovery.

b) Connect to Nature

Purpose: Embody Mrigashira's wandering and inquisitive essence.

Take a walk in a forest, park, or natural area, and allow yourself to wander freely. Observe the patterns of nature—leaves, trails, or even animals. Reflect on an incident in your life, or anyone else's where exploration leads to unexpected discoveries.

c) Perform a Service

Purpose: Share Mrigashira's spirit of seeking and connection with others.

Help someone search for an answer or solution, whether it's offering guidance on a problem or helping them research something important to them. Your support can be a light on their path. Do not expect anything in return.

"The search for meaning begins with a question, but the answer is always found within."

LUNAR MANSION 6: ARDRA

The cosmos whispered a story older than time, a tale etched in the fiery heart of a dying star. ***Betelgeuse***[*] **(Alpha Orionis)**, a celestial giant in the constellation Orion, flickered in the night sky, its crimson glow both a warning and a promise. Its essence embodied a paradox —a beacon of chaos and transformation, a tear drop suspended in eternity.

The ancients had read Ardra's secrets in the heavens, assigning it a symbol—a **teardrop**, shimmering with emotional turbulence, ruled by the shadowy influence of ***Rahu***[*] **(North Node)**. Its corresponding zodiac realm lay under the dominion of **Gemini (lord - Mercury)**, the sign of duality, curiosity, and relentless inquiry.

But Betelgeuse was no mere star. It was a cosmic mirror, reflecting a spiritual truth whispered by sages and sung by the winds of the universe: **"In the storm's eye lies clarity. Let emotional chaos and tears cleanse and reveal your truest self."**

In its pulsating light, the struggles of transformation unfolded—a dance of fire and shadow, where emotional turmoil was not a foe but a guide. Here began the journey —into the storm, into the heart of chaos, where one could find not destruction, but the light of their truest being.

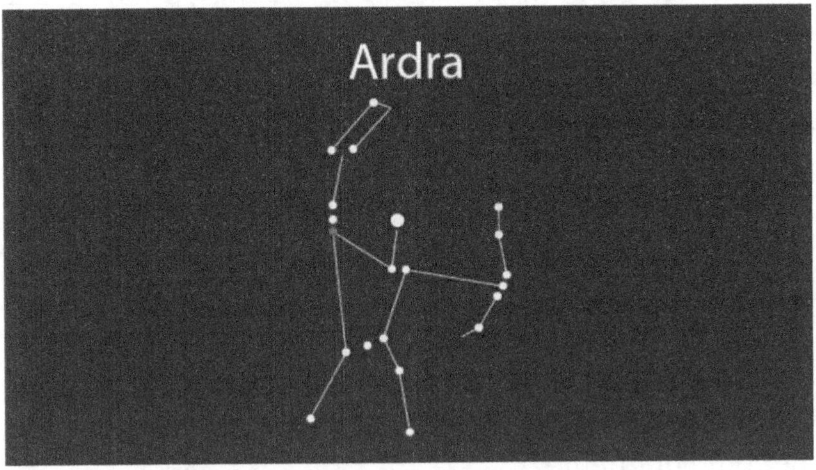

Image Source: https://popularvedicscience.com/astrology/ardra-nakshatra

The Tale of *Rudra** and the Storm of Tears

Context for Readers

In Indian mythology, the gods embody not only creation and preservation but also transformation and destruction. Rudra, a fierce aspect of Shiva, symbolizes the power of chaos and destruction to strip away illusions and bring renewal. Unlike destructive forces in many other cultural myths that often represent pure malevolence, Rudra's storms cleanse and awaken, paving the way for growth and clarity.

This myth-inspired story reflects the essence of Ardra Nakshatra, a lunar mansion associated with transformation through chaos. The storm is a metaphor for life's upheavals that challenge comfort and stagnation, urging individuals to confront their fears, embrace change, and rediscover their inner strength. For those unfamiliar with Indian mythology, Rudra's tale serves as a universal metaphor for how turmoil can catalyze personal growth.

The Story

The heavens were restless. Rudra, the fierce and tempestuous aspect of Shiva, paced along the edges of his domain, his very presence unsettling the ether. Known as the destroyer of illusions and lord of storms, Rudra was both feared and revered. He had learnt the futility of eternal pursuit, yet, within him, an unease lingered—one he could not name.

On Mount *Kailash**, where the winds whispered ancient truths, *Brahma** approached. "Why do you hold back your storms, Rudra? The Earth drowns not in water but in stagnation. The people have lost themselves to complacency and apathy."

Rudra turned his smoldering gaze to Brahma. "My storms destroy, Brahma. They uproot, they raze, they tear apart. How can destruction unleashed by me bring clarity to the creatures of the Earth?"

"Because destruction is the first act of renewal," Brahma replied, his voice like the flow of a quiet river. "It is not chaos alone that you bring, but transformation. Go, Rudra. The Earth awaits."

With reluctant resolve, Rudra descended.

The kingdom he found was no wasteland of war or famine, but its silence was deafening. Rivers lay motionless, the air hung stale, and its people lived in a dull haze of hollow contentment. Their lives, though extremely comfortable with all sorts of materialistic possessions, lacked color, meaning, and fire.

Rudra did not announce himself. His arrival was marked by a subtle shift: a whisper of wind, a flicker of unease. Soon, the skies darkened, the winds howled, and the first cracks of thunder tore across the heavens.

The storm broke with violent beauty. Rain lashed the earth, rivers surged, and winds clawed at the very foundations of the planet. People fled, clutching their possessions, their faces pale with fear. Rudra's tears fell with the rain, a torrent of sorrow for a world that had forgotten how to dream.

Amid the chaos, one figure moved against the tide. Arani, a young woman with eyes as fierce as the storm, ventured out. While others clung to their comforts, Arani had always felt a void in the stillness of her world. Now, in the storm's fury, she felt something stir within her—a challenge she had unknowingly yearned for.

The rain stung her skin, made her gait unsteady, but she pressed forward, her voice cutting through the wind. "Stormlord, I know you are here! Show yourself!"

The storm paused, as if startled. From its roiling center, a figure emerged, vast and imposing, with eyes like molten fire. Rudra's presence was both terrifying and magnetic.

"Why do you walk into the storm?" he asked, his voice the growl of distant thunder.

"Because stillness in the form of stagnation has brought

me nothing," Arani said, her voice steady despite the gale. "If chaos can reveal what lies beyond this void, I want to face it."

Rudra's expression shifted, his gaze searching hers. Then, with a sweep of his hand, the winds around her quieted. "Step into the storm's eye," he said. "Face what you fear most."

Arani closed her eyes and stepped forward. The storm closed around her like a living thing, its roar deafening, its force overwhelming. Fear clawed at her, memories surged—failures, attachments, losses, desires and illusions she had long clung to. Tears poured freely for hours, mingling with the rain.

And then, as suddenly as it had begun, there was silence.

She opened her eyes to find herself in the storm's heart. Here, amidst the chaos, was clarity. The howling winds became whispers of truth, the blinding rain a cleansing embrace. Arani felt her burdens crumble, revealing a self she had never truly seen before—a self-unbound, clear, and alive.

When the storm passed after days, the world had transformed. The destruction had made it unrecognizable. Yet, the old rivers rushed with renewed vigor, the air was crisp with promise, and the people, though shaken, began to rebuild—not with desperation, but with purpose. The kingdom hummed with life, as if Rudra's storm had reawakened its soul.

Arani stood among them, changed. Where once she felt yearning, now there was strength. Her voice carried a new authority as she rallied the people to embrace the renewal left in the storm's wake.

From the horizon, Rudra watched. After a long time, the unease in his heart had diffused. He had torn apart what was stagnant and revealed what was waiting to grow.

"Thank you," Arani whispered, sensing his presence. "For the storm."

Rudra smiled faintly, his gaze softened. "The storm was not just for the world—it was also for you. Clarity lies not in avoiding chaos but in walking through it."

After weeks, as Rudra ascended back to the heavens, he looked once more at the flourishing Earth below and the fierce light in Arani's eyes. The storm had ended, but its purpose had just begun.

Moral of the Story

Chaos is not the enemy; it is a force of transformation. In the midst of destruction lies the opportunity to rebuild, to awaken, and to find clarity. By facing the storm, we discover our truest selves.

Modern-Day Relevance

In a world where comfort and predictability often lull us into complacency, chaos can feel terrifying. Yet, as Ardra teaches, it is through upheaval that we grow and transform.

> Professionally: A sudden job loss or career shift can appear daunting at first, but it can also be a chance to rediscover purpose and realign with personal goals.

Personally: Life's unexpected storms—breakups, losses, or failures—can break illusions and reveal what truly matters.

Spiritually: Chaos can manifest as inner turmoil or existential questions, shaking the foundation of one's beliefs. Facing these "storms" often leads to profound clarity and spiritual growth.

Ardra's energy urges us to embrace the storm, not as destruction, but as a path to clarity and transformation. Through the storm's eye, we find who we truly are.

Real-Life Analogies for the New Seekers

1. The Shattering of a Vase:

Imagine a vase you've had for years. It holds sentimental value, but it's chipped, dull, and no longer serves its purpose. One day, it falls and shatters. At first, you're devastated. But then you realize you can create something entirely new—a mosaic using its fragments, more beautiful and meaningful than the vase ever was.

Lesson: Chaos (the breaking of the vase) leads to clarity (realizing its outdated value) and transformation (creating a mosaic). Like Rudra's storm, it forces you to confront what's broken and repurpose it into something greater.

---

2. Starting Over After a Career Setback:

Consider someone who loses their job

unexpectedly. Initially, they feel lost and overwhelmed, questioning their worth and direction. However, this upheaval pushes them to reassess their skills and passions. They may find clarity about what truly matters and embark on a career aligned with their purpose, which they would never have pursued without the job loss.

Lesson: Like Rudra's storm, the chaos of losing stability reveals inner strength and clarity, leading to renewal and a stronger sense of self.

Rudra's story and Arani's transformation remind us that chaos is not the end but a powerful force for renewal. Whether it's a broken vase, a career change, or an emotional upheaval, embracing the storm rather than fleeing from it reveals clarity, strength, and purpose.

Practical Exercises for the Lunar Mansion

1. Visualization: The Eye of the Storm

Close your eyes and imagine yourself standing in the midst of a fierce storm. The winds roar, the sky flashes with lightning, and chaos surrounds you. As you breathe deeply, a calm eye of the storm forms around you. Within this stillness, you find clarity, courage, and your truest self, unaffected by the chaos.

2. Journaling Prompt

Write about a recent chaotic or challenging situation in your life.

How did you react?

What lessons did you uncover within the experience?

Reflect on a moment when you found peace or clarity amidst difficulty. What can you learn from that?

3. Action for the Day

Embrace a task or activity you've been avoiding due to fear or discomfort. Whether it's confronting a problem, speaking your truth, or organizing a chaotic space, face it with the intention of finding growth and clarity within the process.

Advanced Exercises to Harness the Energy of Ardra

a) Meditation with Sound

Purpose: Channel Ardra's transformative energy.

Meditate for 15 minutes to the sound of a thunderstorm or rolling thunder. Envision the storm washing away chaos, leaving clarity and transformation in its wake.

b) Connect to Nature

Purpose: Align with Ardra's raw and cleansing essence.

Spend time outdoors during or after rain, feeling the water's transformative power. Let the rain or its remnants on the ground cleanse your thoughts and remind you of nature's ability to create clarity after chaos.

c) Perform a Service

Purpose: Transform someone else's chaos into clarity.

Help a friend or colleague who is overwhelmed, whether it's assisting them in organizing tasks, offering emotional support, or sharing insights to help them navigate their storm. Your guidance can be their eye of calm. Do not expect anything in return.

"Chaos is not destruction but transformation; it clears the path for your truest lessons to emerge."

LUNAR MANSION 7: PUNARVASU

The night sky shimmered like a storyteller's canvas, where the twin stars **Castor and Pollux (Alpha Geminorum and Beta Geminorum)** marked the realm of **Punarvasu**. Their light, steady and timeless, carried the essence of **renewal and rebirth**, reflected in the **quiver of arrows**—the nakshatra's enduring symbol.

Ruled by **Jupiter**, the bringer of hope and expansion, Punarvasu whispers of cycles that cradle life itself. **"Embrace life's cycles. Every ending cradles a beginning, every loss a renewal."** The zodiac pairing of **Gemini** and **Cancer (Mercury/Moon)** which oversees Punarvasu, adds intellect's spark and nurture's balm, a reminder that balance lies at the heart of transformation.

Beneath these stars, the universe gently repeats its promise: no matter how many arrows are let loose, the quiver is never empty. In life's endless rhythm, renewal waits patiently, ready to unfold.

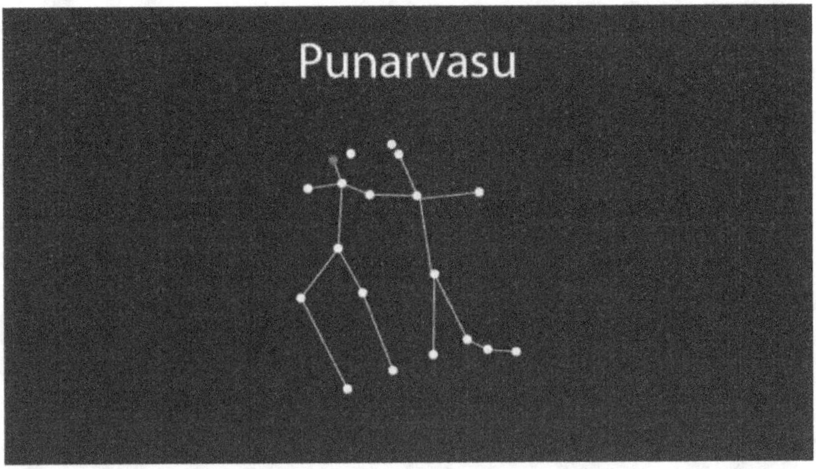

Image Source: https://popularvedicscience.com/astrology/Punarvasu-nakshatra

The Tale of Ahalya: A Journey of Renewal

Context for Readers

Indian mythology often uses allegorical tales involving gods, mortals, and sages to explore universal human experiences. The story of Ahalya, a woman cursed into a stone and later liberated by the divine touch of Prince Rama, is one such narrative. It appears in the Indian epic *Ramayana*[*] and symbolizes the cyclical nature of life—falling into illusion, enduring consequences, and finding redemption.

Ahalya, created as a symbol of perfection, represents the human condition: beauty, flaw, and renewal. Her story highlights that through acceptance and self-awareness, we can overcome even the most immobilizing guilt or stagnation. It reflects the universal truth that endings often lead to beginnings, offering infinite opportunities for transformation.

For readers unfamiliar with Indian mythology, Ahalya's tale can be seen as an allegory for navigating life's mistakes and finding renewal through self-discovery.

The Story

The dense forest hummed with life. Its whispers were a melody only the trees could comprehend. In the heart of this sacred grove stood the hermitage of *Gautama**, a sage whose wisdom bridged the mortal and the divine. His wife, Ahalya, was a creation of unparalleled grace, shaped by Brahma's own hands. Her beauty was revered as a miracle, her form a symbol of perfection. Yet beneath this flawless exterior, many questions stirred.

Ahalya often sat alone, her gaze lost in the dappled light filtering through the forest canopy. "Is this my life's purpose—just to be admired for my looks?" she wondered, her heart heavy. Celebrated for her beauty, she felt her deeper self unseen, unheard. While Gautama's mind remained lost in the glory of eternal truth, she searched for meaning, but no answers came. Her life felt suspended, as if she were a figure etched into stone.

One morning, the forest grew strangely still. The birds fell silent, and the air thickened with an unseen presence. Indra, king of the gods, watched Ahalya from afar. His admiration for her beauty was darkened by desire. "How can such perfection remain hidden here, with a sage who has no value for such a miraculous beauty?" he thought. Disguising himself as Gautama, Indra approached her.

"Ahalya," he said, his tone a mirror of her husband's calm authority. "I have returned."

She hesitated. The familiarity in his voice was almost comforting, but there was something—an undercurrent she could not name. Her restless heart, longing for recognition, silenced her doubts. She allowed herself to believe in the illusion, her vulnerability blinding her to its deceit as she spent time with Indra.

When Gautama returned, the truth unraveled like a storm. His fury burned, sharp and unrelenting. "You were blinded by illusion, Ahalya," he declared. "May you find clarity in stillness." With those words, he cursed her to turn into a stone, bound to the earth she had walked so freely.

The grove enveloped her statue as the seasons passed. Vines wove over her stony form, the forest reclaiming her. At first, her mind spiraled with anguish. "Why did I not see? Why did I falter?" She wrestled with her guilt, each thought heavier than the curse itself. The world continued around her, indifferent to her turmoil.

But time, vast and patient, began its quiet work. The forest lived its cycles around her—trees shed their leaves only to bloom again, rivers receded and swelled with the rhythm of rain. After many many years of observing the changes around her, she started to notice. Slowly, she softened. Her rigid thoughts began to loosen. "The forest does not grieve its changes," she reflected. "Why should I?"

Years became centuries, and with each cycle, she surrendered a little more. What had once felt like punishment began to feel like pause, an interlude in an endless journey. She was no longer a prisoner of her guilt; she became a part of the forest's rhythm.

One day, the forest stirred. Footsteps broke its silence—measured, deliberate. Rama, prince of *Ayodhya**, entered the grove with his brother Lakshmana. The air shimmered around him, a quiet energy radiating from his presence. He paused before the statue which now looked like a mere stone.

"This is no ordinary rock," he said, his voice gentle but sure. "It holds a soul ready to awaken."

He knelt, his touch light yet filled with compassion. A warmth spread through the grove, the vines glistening with dew. Slowly, the stone began to glow. Ahalya's form emerged, her figure radiant with not just beauty but an immense strength, her eyes serene. She stepped forward, her spirit unburdened.

Rama spoke, his words a balm. "You are free, Ahalya. But it was not my touch that freed you. It was your journey—your acceptance, your forgiveness, your surrender to the cycle of renewal."

As she walked through the grove, the vines that had once bound her blossomed into delicate flowers. The air filled with their fragrance, and the forest seemed to exhale in celebration. Rama and Lakshmana watched her from afar, their smiles reflecting the peace she now carried.

In time, Ahalya became a guide to those lost in guilt and despair. Sages and seekers came to her for wisdom, and she shared what the forest had taught her. "Your beauty," she would say, "is not in perfection but in your ability to embrace life's cycles, in accepting that everything rises and falls, whether it is an emotion in your heart or a mighty emperor. Every ending cradles a beginning, every loss a renewal."

And as her words spread, the grove she once called a prison became a sanctuary, a place where many came to learn the art of renewal.

Moral of the Story

Every loss is a step toward renewal. By embracing life's cycles with acceptance and grace, we discover that endings are not final—they are merely transitions to new beginnings.

Modern-Day Relevance

In today's fast-paced world, guilt and regret often trap us in the past, preventing renewal. Ahalya's story reminds us to:

> Professionally: Feeling stuck in a role or career can feel immobilizing, like Ahalya's stone form. But taking time to reflect and embrace change can lead to opportunities that resonate with your true self.
>
> Personally: After a personal failure or relationship breakdown, guilt can paralyze us. Ahalya's story reminds us to forgive ourselves, learn, and allow new connections to bloom.
>
> Spiritually: For those new to spiritual practice, moments of doubt or stagnation may arise. Like Ahalya, recognize these as part of the cycle,

trusting that renewal and clarity will come with persistence.

Punarvasu's energy calls us to trust the cycles of life, finding renewal and rebirth not in running from change but in embracing it.

Real-Life Analogies for the New Seekers

1. The Caterpillar and the Butterfly

    Imagine a caterpillar spinning itself into a cocoon. For days, it remains in complete stillness, seemingly lifeless. To the outside observer, it might appear as though the caterpillar's journey has ended. Yet, within the cocoon, a profound transformation is taking place. When the time is right, the caterpillar emerges as a butterfly—renewed, vibrant, and free.

    Key Lesson: Like Ahalya, our moments of stillness or stagnation are often preparatory stages for personal growth and renewal. What may feel like an end is often the beginning of something greater.

---

2. A Career Setback Leading to a New Path

    Consider someone who loses a long-held job. At first, the loss feels devastating, akin to a "curse" that freezes their progress. However, over time, as they reflect on their passions and explore new opportunities, they find a career path that aligns more deeply with their values. This new phase brings fulfillment they never imagined.

Key Lesson: Just as Ahalya embraced her stillness to find renewal, setbacks in life can serve as opportunities to pause, reflect, and realign with our true purpose.

Ahalya's journey teaches us that life's pauses and mistakes are not permanent setbacks but essential parts of the cycles of growth and renewal. By accepting and learning from these phases, we prepare ourselves for new beginnings, greater clarity, and lasting peace.

Practical Exercises for the Lunar Mansion

1. Visualization: The Cycle of Renewal

Close your eyes and imagine standing at the edge of a vast, still lake under a starry sky. As you drop a stone into the water, ripples form, expanding outward and one ending and another forming. With each ripple, visualize an ending in your life giving way to a new beginning, as the lake reflects the ever-renewing cycles of existence.

2. Journaling Prompt

Reflect on a recent ending or loss in your life.

What did this chapter teach you?

How can you embrace the possibilities that this ending has created?

Write about a time when you found renewal or a fresh start after a difficult phase. What steps helped you move forward?

3. Action for the Day

Weeding out some leaves or trimming some plants in your garden—or tearing out an old page from your journal which you randomly scribbled on. Let this act remind you of the natural cycles of endings and beginnings, and nurture it as a symbol of renewal in your life.

Advanced Exercises to Harness the Energy of Punarvasu

a) Meditation with Sound

Purpose: Align with Punarvasu's energy of renewal and rebirth.

Meditate for 15 minutes to the sound of gentle river currents. Imagine the flow renewing your energy and creating space for new beginnings.

b) Connect to Nature

Purpose: Embrace Punarvasu's cyclical and nurturing essence.

Spend time in a space that reflects renewal, such as a garden or a meadow after rain. Observe how nature renews itself and reflect on how you can do the same in your own life.

c) Perform a Service

Purpose: Share the energy of renewal with someone else.

Help someone rebuild or restart—whether it's

assisting a friend in reorganizing their home, encouraging a colleague facing challenges, or simply listening to someone in need of a fresh perspective. Your support can inspire renewal in their journey. Do not expect anything in return.

"Life is a cycle of endings and beginnings; what you lose today is the seed of tomorrow's beginning."

LUNAR MANSION 8: PUSHYA

Beneath the nurturing light of **Gamma and Delta Cancri (Asellus Australis)** lies the sacred realm of **Pushya**, a celestial harbor of **nourishment and spiritual growth**. Its emblem, the **Cow's Udder or Lotus**, reflects the life-giving essence of this nakshatra, where Saturn's steady hand governs with discipline and purpose.

Anchored in the **zodiac sign of Cancer (ruled by the Moon)**, Pushya marries **Saturn's (nakshatra lord of Pushya)** resilience with the Moon's tender care, creating a perfect blend of wisdom and compassion. Together, they remind us that true growth thrives in the soil of selflessness, where the act of nurturing others becomes a pathway to personal nourishment.

Pushya's enduring promise lies in its cosmic message: **"Growth blooms from wisdom and compassion. Nurture others, and you will be nourished."** Under its watchful stars, the universe unfolds a simple truth—by giving freely, we are replenished, and by caring deeply, we find our own strength renewed.

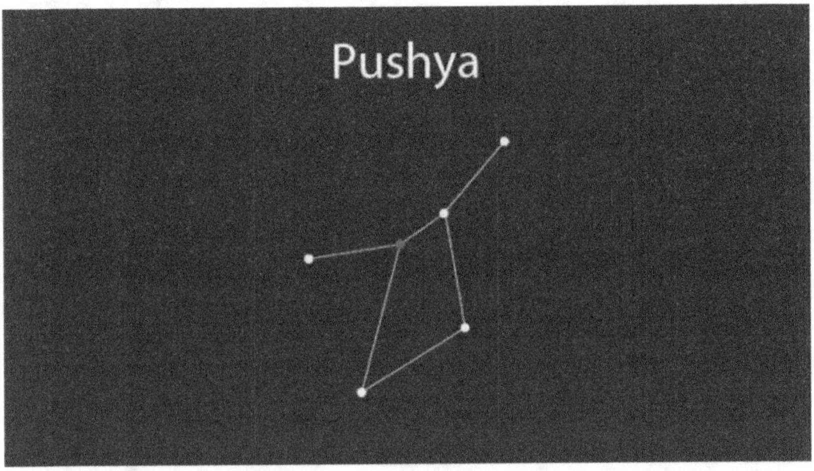

Image Source: https://popularvedicscience.com/astrology/pushya-nakshatra

The Tale of *Brihaspati and Pushya: The Milk of the Cosmos**

Context for Readers

In Indian mythology, the gods, known as the *Devas**, embody various forces of nature and principles that sustain the universe. Each deity has a unique role—*Indra** (very similar to Thor) governs rain and storms, *Agni** presides over fire and energy, and *Varuna** oversees water and the cosmic order. Together, these gods are meant to work in harmony, ensuring the balance of creation.

However, like humans, even the gods are susceptible to pride, ambition, and discord, which can disrupt cosmic harmony. At such times, figures of great wisdom, like Brihaspati, the celestial teacher and guru of the gods, intervene to restore balance. Brihaspati represents wisdom, compassion, and the higher principles that guide both divine and mortal beings.

This myth-inspired story also introduces *Kamadhenu**, the divine cow revered in Indian mythology as the ultimate source of nourishment and prosperity, just like the symbol of Pushya and its cosmic message. Kamadhenu symbolizes selfless giving, abundance, and the nurturing aspects of the universe. Her milk is not just physical nourishment but a representation of the life force that sustains all existence.

Through the narrative of Brihaspati and Kamadhenu, this myth explores profound themes of humility, sharing, and the true meaning of nourishment—ideas that transcend cultural boundaries and resonate universally. Whether in the cosmic realms or our daily lives, the act of giving is central to restoring harmony and purpose.

The Story

The celestial realms rippled with unrest. The gods, once the guardians of cosmic harmony, now stood fractured. Indra, the king of the heavens, amassed wealth to secure his dominion. Agni, the god of fire, burned with the desire for unrivaled fame. Varuna, the lord of water, hoarded his resources, refusing to let them flow freely. Their discord echoed across creation, and the Earth bore its strain, trembling under their growing neglect.

In the midst of this turmoil, Brihaspati, the wise teacher of the gods, observed silently. He saw the cracks forming within his students, not just in their unity but even in their purpose. "They have strayed from their essence," he thought, his heart heavy. "Their power is meant to nourish, yet they wield it only for themselves."

One night, under the boughs of a great celestial tree, Brihaspati sank into deep meditation, seeking guidance. A vision emerged from the stillness—a golden cow, radiant as a thousand suns, its gentle presence exuding an unending stream of nourishment. Kamadhenu, the divine source of sustenance, spoke in his vision: "The gods must remember their purpose. Take my milk and let them learn the truth of nurturing through humility."

When Brihaspati awoke, the vision lingered like a soft hum in the air. Without hesitation, he descended to the earthly realm, his resolve unwavering. His journey was not an easy one—through blistering deserts, over frostbitten peaks, and across dense forests. After many days and nights, in a serene meadow untouched by the clamor of the world, he found her. Kamadhenu stood gracefully, her golden coat shimmering under the sun.

"Kamadhenu," Brihaspati called, bowing deeply, "the heavens are in disarray. The gods have forgotten their roles as nurturers. Will you lend me your milk to guide them back?"

Kamadhenu turned her gaze upon him, her deep eyes reflecting boundless compassion. "My milk holds the essence of life itself," she said. "But it will yield its blessings only to those who seek it with humility and the intent to uplift other creatures. This is your test: bring my milk to them, but ensure it is not hoarded or corrupted. Begin with Indra, then Agni, and finally Varuna."

With reverence, Brihaspati filled a golden vessel with Kamadhenu's milk and returned to the celestial plane. The gods had been summoned by their teacher, each drawn by the promise of unparalleled power.

He approached Indra first. The king of the gods seized the vessel greedily. "This milk will make my kingdom eternal, unassailable," he declared, his pride gleaming. But as the milk touched his lips, its golden luster faded, and the liquid soured into bitterness. Indra spat it out in frustration. "Why does it reject me?"

Brihaspati's voice was calm, yet firm. "You seek to hoard what is meant to be shared. True power uplifts others, not just the self."

Next, Brihaspati turned to Agni. The god of fire, his ambition glowing fiercely, took the vessel with trembling hands. "This milk will make my flames everlasting, consuming all," he boasted. Yet as he drank, the milk evaporated, leaving him thirstier than before. "Why does it not sustain me?" he demanded.

Brihaspati replied, "A fire that does not warm or illuminate is hollow. True strength lies in service, not in destruction."

Finally, Brihaspati approached Varuna. The god of water, guarded and wary after seeing the fate of the other two, accepted the vessel reluctantly. He sipped the milk, and to his surprise, it transformed into a cool nectar, rejuvenating him. The change was not just in the liquid but in his heart. For the first time, Varuna saw his hoarded wealth as a burden rather than a treasure. "This is not mine to keep," he murmured, offering the milk back.

Moved by Varuna's humility, the gods began to share the milk among themselves. Its essence flowed freely, blazing a trail of renewal across the heavens. As they drank, their pride dissolved, and their divine roles became clear once more. Indra's might became a shield for creation, Agni's fire a guiding light, and Varuna's waters a source of life. The cosmos regained its balance, and the Earth thrived under their united care.

Kamadhenu appeared, her voice resonating like a gentle hymn. "You and your students have passed the test, Brihaspati. My milk will forever flow where wisdom and compassion reside."

Brihaspati smiled, his gaze sweeping over the restored harmony. "To nurture others is to nurture ourselves. In giving, we grow. In sharing, we find abundance."

And in the glow of the celestial realm, the gods remembered their place in the eternal cycle of creation: as stewards, not masters, of the universe's boundless gifts.

Moral of the Story

True nourishment lies in giving and uplifting others. Wisdom and compassion are the roots of growth, and when we share selflessly, we create harmony within and around us.

Modern-Day Relevance

In today's world, where individualism and competition often overshadow community and connection, this story offers timeless lessons:

Professionally: In competitive environments, leaders and team members often focus on individual achievement. This story reminds us that real success comes when resources, ideas, and support are shared for the collective good.

Personally: In relationships, true connection and growth happen when individuals nurture each other selflessly rather than seeking only personal gain. Compassion creates bonds that sustain everyone involved.

Spiritually: The act of giving—whether it's knowledge, kindness, or resources—connects us to something greater. By uplifting others, we find our own spiritual growth and fulfillment.

Real-Life Analogies for the New Seekers

1. Teamwork in the Workplace:

Imagine a workplace where team members prioritize their own success over the group's goals. Projects stagnate, and morale declines. However, when a leader like Brihaspati steps in to remind everyone of their shared purpose, the team begins to collaborate. Individuals contribute selflessly, and the entire team thrives, achieving success together.

Key Lesson: Just as Kamadhenu's milk nourishes only when shared, mutual support and collaboration lead to collective and personal growth.

2. Parenting and Caregiving:

A parent spends their time and energy nurturing their child, often sacrificing their own comforts. While the parent gives selflessly, they find deep fulfillment in their child's growth and happiness. This mirrors how sharing and caring for others naturally brings nourishment to one's own spirit.

Key Lesson: Like Kamadhenu's milk, the act of nurturing others replenishes and enriches the giver.

The story of Pushya teaches that the path to spiritual and personal growth lies in selflessness. When we nourish others, we align ourselves with the natural flow of the universe, discovering harmony and fulfillment in the process. Just as the gods found their true roles by sharing Kamadhenu's milk, we too can find clarity and purpose by embracing compassion and generosity.

Practical Exercises for the Lunar Mansion

1. Visualization: The Tree of Nourishment

Close your eyes and imagine yourself as a tree rooted firmly in rich soil. Visualize your roots drawing strength and nourishment from the Earth, while your branches reach toward the sky, providing shade, fruit, and oxygen to those around you. Feel the balance between receiving sustenance and giving back to the world.

2. Journaling Prompt

Reflect on the areas of your life where you give

nourishment to others—emotionally, spiritually, or physically.

> How does this make you feel?
>
> Are there areas where you need to better nurture yourself to continue supporting others?

Write about a time when compassion or kindness from someone else nourished your spirit. How can you pass this on to others?

3. Action for the Day

Engage in an act of nurturing, whether it's cooking a healthy meal for yourself or someone else, offering emotional support to a loved one, or helping someone in need. Let this act reinforce the balance between giving and receiving.

Advanced Exercises to Harness the Energy of Pushya

a) Meditation with Sound

> Purpose: Connect with Pushya's nurturing and spiritual growth energy.
>
> Meditate for 15 minutes to harmonized bell tones layered with soft chimes. Feel the nourishing vibrations spreading wisdom and compassion within you.

b) Connect to Nature

> Purpose: Embody Pushya's nurturing essence.
>
> Spend time with a large tree, observing its strength

and the shelter it provides to birds, animals, and humans. Reflect on how you can serve as a source of support and growth for those around you.

c) Perform a Service

Purpose: Share Pushya's energy of nourishment with others.

Volunteer at a food bank, cook for someone who is unwell, or donate resources to support a local cause. Acts of nourishment in any form enhance your connection to Pushya's compassionate energy. Do not expect anything in return.

"To nourish others is to nourish yourself; compassion is the soil where all growth begins."

LUNAR MANSION 9: ASHLESHA

Ashlesha coils its mysteries among the stars. Anchored within the constellation of **Hydra**, its astral companions —**Epsilon, Delta, Eta, Rho, and Sigma Hydrae**— glimmer with an enigmatic allure. Like the **serpent** they symbolize, their light winds through the heavens, whispering secrets of **introspection and self-transformation**.

At the heart of **Ashlesha**, the coiled **Serpent**, lies the wisdom of Mercury, its planetary lord. This symbol, both revered and feared, embodies the tension between attachment and liberation. In its corresponding zodiac sign, **Cancer (ruled by Moon)**, the serpent's energy finds balance between intuition's pull and emotions that bind.

The spiritual theme of **introspection, intuition, and self-transformation** unfurls in the cosmic message: **"Introspection coupled with intuition breaks the chains of attachment, freeing the soul for true growth."** It is a call to turn inward, to harness the power of the serpent's coil not for entrapment, but for release, shedding what no longer serves and stepping boldly into the light of growth.

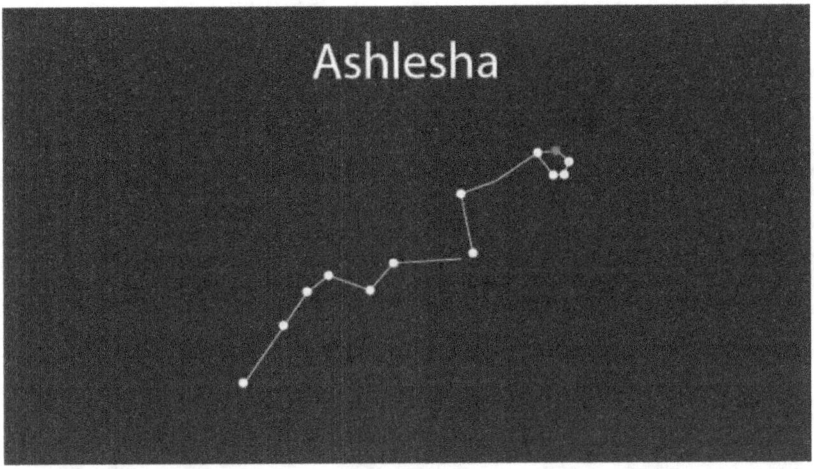

Image Source: https://popularvedicscience.com/astrology/ashlesha-nakshatra

The Tale of *Vasuki** and the Hidden Poison

Context for Readers

In Indian mythology, the cosmos and life are often represented as intertwined, with gods, demons, and celestial beings serving as allegories for human virtues, struggles, and growth. One of the most profound stories is the Churning of the Ocean (*Samudra Manthan**), symbolizing the effort to extract wisdom from life's challenges.

At the center of this tale is Vasuki, the king of serpents, who reluctantly plays a pivotal role in churning the ocean. His journey—from resistance and pride to self-confrontation and transformation—embodies the universal truth that growth often requires facing our darkest fears. This myth-inspired story reminds us that only by confronting our hidden flaws and attachments can we free ourselves for genuine growth.

The Story

There was a time when gods and demons faced an unprecedented crisis. The strength of the Gods was diminishing and demons were becoming stronger, yet lacking any drive and direction. The cosmic ocean, the cradle of life and vitality, had grown lifeless. Its waters no longer infused energy in creatures but lay stagnant and heavy, suffocating the balance of creation. Without *amrita**, the nectar of immortality hidden deep within, even the gods would eventually succumb to decay.

Desperate, the gods turned to *Vishnu**, the preserver of the universe. His gaze, calm yet piercing, rested upon the gathered deities. "The nectar lies buried in the depths," Vishnu explained. "To retrieve it, you must churn the ocean. But such a feat requires strength beyond your own. You will need a mountain to become the churning rod, but more importantly you will need Vasuki, the king of serpents, to serve as the churning rope."

Far beneath the surface of the earth, Vasuki ruled the *Nagas** (serpents) with wisdom tempered by a fierce pride. His shimmering scales and towering presence were symbols of his authority, yet within him, there was no peace. Vasuki carried a burden, hidden even from himself —a pride so potent it tethered him to his power, trapping him in a cage of his own making.

When the gods descended to his subterranean palace, Vasuki looked at them with suspicion. "You ask me to coil myself around a mountain? To be a tool in your hands?" His voice hissed through the chamber. "I am a king, not a servant or a tool."

Vishnu's response was steady, like a river cutting through stone. "Greatness lies not in what you possess, Vasuki, but in what you overcome. This is not a task of servitude—it could become your path to transcendence."

The words struck something deep within the serpent king, igniting a spark of doubt in the fortress of his pride. Reluctantly, he agreed, not out of submission but with a faint, unspoken hope that this might release him from the perpetual restlessness inside him.

Coiling himself around Mount *Mandara**, Vasuki stretched his mighty form, his scales glinting under the celestial light. The gods and demons, bound by necessity, joined forces. Gods held Vasuki like a rope on one end and the demons took charge of the other. Together, they churned the ocean with Vasuki as their churning rope. The mountain groaned under the strain, its rocks biting into Vasuki's flesh. Tsunamis rose in rebellion, crashing against the heavens.

Each pull tested Vasuki's resolve. His pride whispered insidious temptations: *Abandon this measly task. You are above this indignity.* Yet beneath the pain and humiliation, something deeper stirred—his intuition cradled a desire to break free from the very pride that bound him. After thousands of years of churning, he began to realize that his pride started to mellow. His introspection indicated that his struggle was not with the gods or the mountain but with himself.

As the churning continued, the ocean yielded treasures of unparalleled beauty: celestial jewels, divine creatures, and wonders that dazzled even the gods. Yet the labor was far from over. From the depths of the ocean, a shadow emerged—a swirling mass of venomous darkness. The poison, *halahala*[*], rose like a monstrous force, its fumes toxifying the air, its touch threatening to dissolve all creation.

The gods and demons recoiled, their faces pale with terror. "The poison will destroy us all!" they cried. The air grew thick, suffocating, and the universe seemed to teeter on the brink of collapse.

Vasuki froze, his form tense as he stared into the poison. He sensed that this was not just a physical threat—it was also a reflection of his own fears and attachments. The venom mirrored the pride, resentment, and chains of identity he had clung to for ages. For the first time, he saw the truth: the poison outside was no different from the poison within.

In that moment of clarity, Vasuki's voice broke through the chaos. "I will not run from this. This poison is mine to endure." His gaze turned to Shiva, the destroyer who had joined the churning. "Take the poison," Vasuki said, his voice steady. "But let me bear its weight. It is my burden to face. As long as the universe lasts, you may distribute the poison amongst the serpents and let them be hated for it."

Shiva, moved by Vasuki's courage, stepped forward. With a calm resolve, Shiva drank the poison, holding it in his throat so it would harm neither him nor the world. The act turned his throat blue, earning him the name *Neelkanth** (The Blue-Throated One). In the ages that followed, this poison in Shiva's throat became the source of the venom that serpents carried.

As the fumes dissipated, Vasuki felt an extraordinary change within. The chains of pride and attachment that had once held him down were gone, replaced by a clarity he had never known. By confronting his fears and embracing his role in rescuing the universe, Vasuki had broken free of the internal venom that had bound him.

After some more churning, the nectar of immortality rose from the ocean, restoring life and harmony to creation. Yet for Vasuki, the true treasure was not the nectar but the transformation within. The struggle had reshaped him, stripping away illusions and revealing the strength born from surrender and introspection.

When Vasuki returned to his palace, the Nagas gazed at him in awe. His once darkened scales now gleamed with a radiant, golden hue. He was no longer just their king—he was a symbol of renewal, a testament to the power of facing one's inner darkness. And all Nagas would become the embodiment of the sacrifice for saving the universe.

The story of Vasuki spread across the ages, a beacon

for sages and seekers alike. His journey taught that the venom within us—the pride, fear, and attachments—must be faced with courage and introspection. Only then can we break free and grow.

For as Vasuki learned, true transformation comes not from running but from standing firm, looking inward, and trusting the quiet voice of intuition that guides us toward freedom.

Moral of the Story

Vasuki's transformation teaches that the greatest battles are often within ourselves. Facing our inner darkness is not a weakness but a courageous act that paves the way for renewal, strength, and liberation. Like Vasuki, every new seeker can turn fear into a source of light by embracing introspection and growth.

Modern-Day Relevance

In today's world, people often avoid self-reflection, fearing the truths they might uncover. Vasuki's story reminds us that:

> Professionally: Confronting personal flaws, such as arrogance or resistance to change, can lead to greater leadership and growth.
>
> Personally: Facing unresolved emotions or past traumas allows for healing and deeper connections with others.
>
> Spiritually: True enlightenment requires acknowledging and transforming the shadows within

Ashlesha's energy teaches us that introspection is not an act of weakness but of immense strength. Only by facing our inner poison can we unlock the path to true growth and transformation

---

Real-Life Analogies for the New Seekers

1. Analogy 1: The Mirror of Feedback

Imagine an employee receiving constructive feedback about their work performance. Initially, they feel defensive, their pride wounded. But upon introspection, they realize the critique highlights areas for improvement they had been avoiding. By embracing this feedback and addressing their shortcomings, they transform into a more competent professional.

Takeaway: Just like Vasuki, we must confront our inner "poison"—be it ego, fear, or attachments—to grow into our potential.

2. Analogy 2: Spring Cleaning the Mind

Think of a cluttered room that hasn't been cleaned for years. It holds items that are no longer useful but remain out of attachment. Cleaning the room requires effort and can stir up dust and discomfort. But once done, the space becomes lighter, open, and inviting for new energy.

Takeaway: Introspection helps us clear mental and emotional clutter, freeing us to invite growth and clarity into our lives.

Practical Exercises for the Lunar Mansion

1. Visualization: Shedding the Old Skin

Close your eyes and picture yourself as a serpent coiled in the depths of a tranquil forest. Imagine shedding your old skin, symbolizing the release of attachments, fears, and outdated patterns. With each breath, feel yourself growing lighter and more liberated as the new, glistening skin emerges, embodying transformation and self-growth.

2. Journaling Prompt

Reflect on a habit, belief, or attachment that no longer serves you.

Why are you holding onto it?

What would life look like without this weight?

Write about a time when letting go of something or someone led to significant personal growth. How can you replicate this in your current life?

3. Action for the Day

Choose one small thing to release today—whether it's an item you no longer need, a task you've been procrastinating on, or an emotional burden. Take an action to let it go, and observe how it creates space for something new.

Advanced Exercises to Harness the Energy of Ashlesha

a) Meditation with Sound

Purpose: Align with Ashlesha's transformative and introspective energy.

Meditate for 15 minutes to the serpentine hissing and soft rattles. Picture these sounds unraveling attachments, helping you transform from within. You may try to imagine a snake shedding its skin and transforming. Stop if you feel uncomfortable.

b) Connect to Nature

Purpose: Embrace Ashlesha's serpentine essence.

Spend time observing reptiles or snakes in their natural habitat, or study their symbolic meaning in nature. Reflect on their ability to adapt, transform, and shed what no longer serves them, drawing inspiration for your own transformation.

c) Perform a Service

Purpose: Share Ashlesha's wisdom of introspection and renewal with others.

Help someone declutter their physical or emotional space. Offer guidance or support to someone looking to let go of the past or embrace change, mirroring Ashlesha's transformative power. Do not expect anything in return.

"Introspection reveals the chains we've forged; liberation begins when we face our reflection."

LUNAR MANSION 10: MAGHA

Beneath the fiery gaze of **Regulus (Alpha Leonis)**, the heart of the Leo constellation, lies the domain of **Magha**. Its presence in the night sky commands reverence, a celestial beacon illuminating the themes of **legacy and duty**. This mansion's symbol, the **throne**, evokes both power and responsibility, underlining its planetary lord, **Ketu (South Node)**, who whispers of the past's unseen threads guiding the present.

Nestled in the Zodiac sign of **Leo (Sun)**, Magha carries the weight of heritage and the warmth of purpose. It calls upon the seeker to embrace not only the glory of action but the profound responsibility it carries—towards the self, the ancestors, and those yet to come.

Its eternal wisdom resounds in the cosmos: **"In every action, honor the roots that hold you and the legacy you create for others."** As Regulus anchors its regal light in the heavens, it asks: How will you wield your throne? For in every choice, the echoes of a lineage are heard, and the seeds of a legacy are sown.

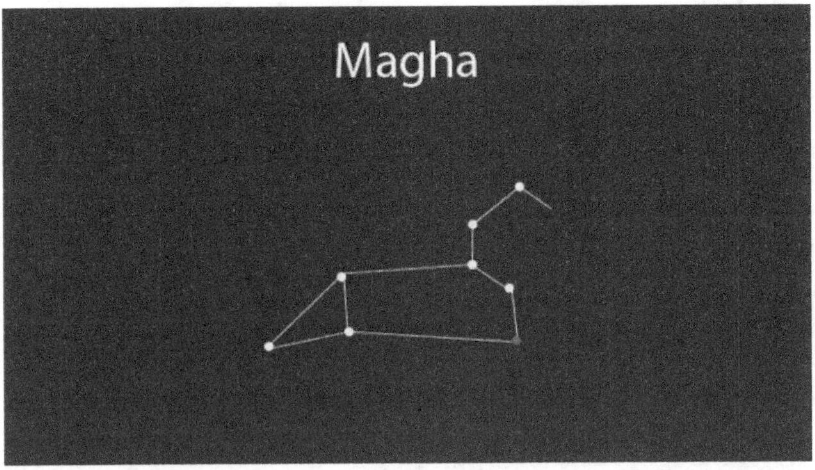

Image Source: https://popularvedicscience.com/astrology/magha-nakshatra

---

The Legacy of Magha: The Guardian of Generations

Context for Readers

In Vedic Astrology, Magha symbolizes the deep connection between our ancestors and the legacy we leave behind. It is associated with the *Pitris**, the spirits of forebears who guide and protect their descendants. The story of King *Raghu** highlights the lesson that true greatness is achieved not through what we acquire but through what we give to honor the past and secure the future.

The Story

The Kingdom of *Kosala**, nestled along the shimmering Sarayu River, was a realm of abundant prosperity. Golden fields stretched to the horizon, the laughter of its people filled the air, and its skies bore the blessings of its ancestors. At the heart of this flourishing kingdom stood King Raghu, a ruler of boundless courage and humility. His reign was a tribute to the legacy of his forebears, marked by fairness and an unwavering devotion to the people.

As twilight painted the land in hues of amber one evening, the palace gates creaked open to admit an elderly figure draped in the simplicity of a life steeped in wisdom.

It was Sage *Vasishtha**, the spiritual guide of the royal family and a seer of truths hidden from mortal eyes. His gaze, though serene, carried a gravity that made Raghu rise to greet him.

"Your Majesty," Vasishtha began, his voice steady yet tinged with sorrow, "your kingdom thrives, but I bring a message from the Pitris—your ancestors. They whisper of a debt left unfulfilled, a balance that must be restored. If left unattended, the roots of this prosperity will dry, and the branches will eventually wither."

Raghu's brow furrowed in concern."What debt, wise one? I have ruled with justice, honored the traditions, and safeguarded the legacy of those who came before me."

Vasishtha inclined his head, his expression softening. "It is a debt not of riches or grain, but of sacrifice. Your ancestors gave of themselves to nurture this kingdom, and now the time has come for you to offer what is most precious to you. Only then will the roots of Kosala's prosperity remain strong."

Raghu straightened, his resolve unshaken. "O wise one ! Tell me what must be done."

The sage led him to the edge of the forest, where the trees whispered secrets to the wind. Before them stood a simple yet sacred altar, adorned with garlands and sanctified by time. "Here you must perform the Pitri *Yajna** (fire ritual for ancestors)," Vasishtha explained. "It is not a mere ritual, but a call to give away that which sustains you most. The fire will reveal the truth."

The fire roared to life as Raghu stood before it, its golden tongues licking the twilight air. His mind churned with questions, but he said nothing, awaiting the revelation. The flames danced, shifting and shimmering until they took form—not of words, but of visions.

He saw the kingdom's richness:overflowing granaries, joyous festivals, and his people unburdened by want. Then, the scenes moved towards the future and the images darkened. The fields dried, the laughter faded, and the land grew barren. A shadow fell over Kosala, suffocating its once-bright spirit.

"What must I do?" Raghu whispered, his voice trembling as the weight of his duty squished him.

The fire did not speak, but the visions sharpened, lingering on the royal treasury—a vault teeming with jewels, coins, and treasures collected over generations. It was more than wealth; it was the lifeblood of the kingdom's strength. The fire's message was clear: "Give away that which sustains you."

For a moment, Raghu faltered. The treasury was not just his wealth; it was the foundation of Kosala's stability. To relinquish it meant plunging into uncertainty. Yet, as the images of a barren Kosala loomed larger, his resolve solidified. He turned to his ministers and commanded, "Empty the treasury. Distribute its riches among the people, the priests, and the sacred rituals of this yajna."

The ministers hesitated, their faces pale with disbelief, but Raghu's gaze allowed no argument. The vaults were emptied, and the treasures poured forth like a river into the hands of the people. The flames of the yajna consumed the offerings, their radiance growing brighter with each passing moment.

In the forest, the chants of the yajna mingled with the cries of the people—not of despair, but of gratitude. They wept not for the gold, but for the gift of a king who valued their future above his own throne. The fire softened to a warm glow, its hunger sated, as the balance was restored.

Raghu stood before the dying embers, the heaviness in his chest giving way to quiet clarity. "Have I done enough, wise one?" he asked, turning to Vasishtha.

The sage's eyes gleamed with approval. "You have done more than honor the past, my king. You have taught your people the true essence of legacy—that it is not in what we hold but in what we give. This act will echo through generations, shaping the future of Kosala long after you are gone."

Years passed, and Raghu's descendants faced trials of their own. When the weight of leadership bore down upon them, they looked to his sacrifice as their guiding light. His act of selflessness became a cornerstone of the Raghu dynasty's greatness, a story whispered in the halls of Kosala and sung by its people. There were times when the kingdom faced siege, its walls trembling under the weight of invading forces for years together. There were wars which lasted decades but the soldiers stood steadfast, waging relentless battles against those who sought to shatter Kosala's prosperity. Yet, in every moment of peril, the people of Kosala rose as one. With unwavering resolve, they poured their wealth, labor, hearts and even lives, into replenishing the royal treasury and fortifying the armed forces, embodying the legacy of selflessness that King Raghu had etched into their very spirit. The kingdom thrived, its roots nourished by a legacy not of gold but of giving. "In every action, honor the roots that hold you and the legacy you create for others." The likes of King Harishchandra and Lord Rama were all descendants of Raghu. His life had become the embodiment of this truth, and his people carried it forward, the unbroken thread of a dynasty woven with duty and devotion.

Moral of the Story

True legacy is built on selflessness and duty. Honoring the roots that sustain us ensures that the branches of our lives and actions bear fruit for generations to come.

Modern-Day Relevance

In a world driven by individual gain, Raghu's story reminds us of the power of legacy and the importance of honoring the past while building a better future.

Professionally: Leaders and entrepreneurs often

face decisions where short-term gains clash with long-term sustainability. Choosing to reinvest profits into employee welfare, innovation, or environmental practices reflects a commitment to legacy over immediate reward.

Personally: Parents working hard to provide opportunities for their children or individuals preserving cultural traditions for future generations embody the values of Magha. Their actions honor the past while securing the future.

Socially: By acknowledging the contributions of those who came before us—whether family, teachers, or mentors—we strengthen our connection to the greater whole and find fulfillment in giving back.

Magha teaches that by honoring the past and embracing our duty to the future, we ensure the continuity of values, harmony, and prosperity. Like King Raghu, we are guardians of the roots that hold us and creators of the legacy that will inspire those who come after.

Real-Life Analogies for the New Seekers

1. Family Tradition and Sacrifice:

Imagine a person inheriting a family business. They work tirelessly to maintain its success, honoring the sacrifices their parents and grandparents made to build it. One day, they face a financial crisis and must choose between holding onto their personal wealth or reinvesting it to save the business and its employees. By choosing the latter, they honor their ancestors' legacy and secure a brighter future for the next generation.

Key Takeaway: Like King Raghu, true wealth lies in giving back to the roots that sustain you, ensuring their strength for those who follow.

---

2. A Teacher's Lasting Impact:

Think of a teacher who dedicates their career to nurturing students' minds. As they approach retirement, they donate their personal library to the school and establish a scholarship fund for underprivileged students. Though they leave the classroom, their contributions continue to shape young lives, leaving an enduring legacy of education and opportunity.

Key Takeaway: Legacy is not measured by what we keep but by what we give to enrich the lives of others, ensuring the continuity of values and knowledge.

True legacy is built through sacrifice and selflessness. It's not the wealth you amass but the wisdom and love you pass on that defines your impact on the world.

Practical Exercises for the Lunar Mansion

1. Visualization: The Throne of Legacy

Close your eyes and imagine yourself seated on a magnificent throne in a vast hall filled with ancestral imagery and energy. Around you are glowing symbols of the legacy you have inherited—values, traditions, and wisdom. Visualize yourself holding a torch that represents your contribution to this legacy, ready to carry it forward with honor and responsibility.

2. Journaling Prompt

Reflect on the legacy you've inherited from your family, community, or mentors.

> What values, traditions, or lessons have shaped you?
>
> How can you honor and build upon this legacy in your own unique way?

Write about the legacy you wish to leave behind. How can your current actions contribute to this vision?

3. Action for the Day

Perform an action that honors your roots or contributes to your legacy. This could be reconnecting with an elder, preserving a family tradition, or starting a project that aligns with your core values and long-term vision.

Advanced Exercises to Harness the Energy of Magha

a) Meditation with Sound

Purpose: Connect with Magha's regal and ancestral energy.

Meditate for 15 minutes to ceremonial drumrolls with conch shell echoes. Envision these sounds honoring your legacy and strengthening your sense of purpose.

b) Connect to Nature

Purpose: Embody Magha's sense of rootedness and honor.

Spend time near an ancient yet good looking building or an ancient tree, symbolizing deep roots and towering strength. Reflect on how your roots, like the tree's, provide stability and nourishment for growth and impact.

c) Perform a Service

Purpose: Honor Magha's legacy by uplifting others.

Help someone connect with their heritage or support a cause that preserves culture, wisdom, or traditions. Acts like documenting family stories or volunteering for community heritage programs align with Magha's energy. Do not expect anything in return.

"Legacy is not built in monuments but in the silent ripple of actions that echo through generations."

LUNAR MANSION 11: PURVA PHALGUNI

The night holds many secrets, but few are as inviting and joyous as Purva Phalguni. Known in the night sky as **Delta Leonis (Zosma)** and **Theta Leonis (Chertan)**, this lunar mansion embodies the warmth of its own ruler **Venus** and the vitality of its zodiac—**Leo's** ruling **Sun**. Its symbol—the **front legs of a bed**—evokes an image of intimacy, rest, and creation, a foundation upon which life's most profound joys unfold.

Purva Phalguni whispers of the essence of life itself: **love, procreation, and celebration**. It teaches us that existence is far more than the sum of our physical experiences. **Life’s vitality is deeply rooted in connection—not just with others, but with the creative forces that express your soul's essence**. Joy, relationships, and creative expression are the pathways to transcendence, allowing you to revel in the miracle of existence.

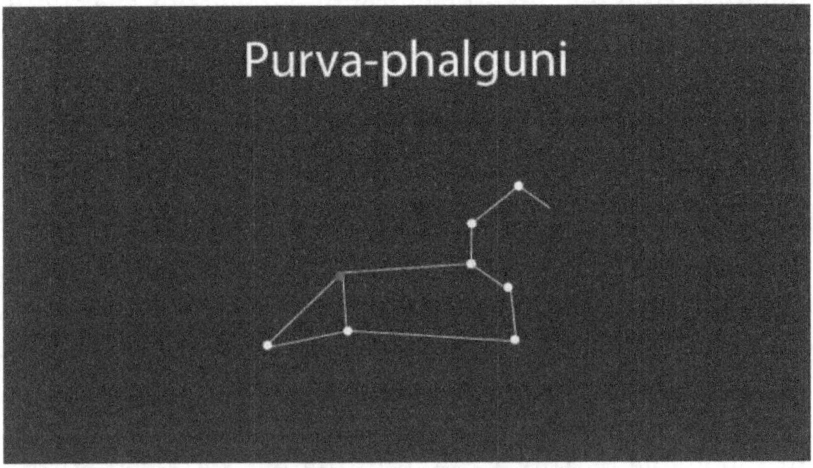

Image Source: https://popularvedicscience.com/astrology/purva-phalguni-nakshatra

---

The Tale of Ushas and the Garden of Joy

The Context

In Indian mythology, Ushas, the goddess of dawn, represents renewal, beauty, and the hope that accompanies every new beginning. She heralds the arrival of the sun, symbolizing vitality and the joy of life.

This myth-inspired story of Ushas illustrates the universal truth that joy and fulfillment come not from individual achievements or solitary endeavors but from shared experiences and meaningful connections. It's a reminder that life's true light shines brightest when it is shared with others.

The Story

The golden hue of dawn stretched across the heavens, casting a gentle glow over Amaravati, the celestial garden where spring had an eternal reign. Flowers of every hue adorned its verdant expanse, their fragrance mingling with the soft hum of flowing streams. In the garden's heart, Ushas, the goddess of dawn, moved with grace, her laughter a melody that brought life to the waking world.

Her light was revered by all—gods, mortals, and celestial beings alike. They hailed her as the harbinger of hope, the radiant force that dispelled darkness each morning. Ushas held such a revered status and carried such an aura of majesty that everyone hesitated to approach her, while she, in turn, had been taught to remain distant, untouchable by those she illuminated. Yet, deep within her luminous presence lay a shadow she could never ignore. Despite her brilliance, Ushas felt distant from the joy she bestowed. Each dawn seemed a gift, only for others, leaving her heart unkindled. "What is the use of light," she often wondered, "if it does not warm the one who carries it?"

That morning, her dance faltered as her thoughts turned inward. She lingered by a stream, its surface reflecting her radiant form. The still water mirrored her unspoken ache —a beauty admired but never truly felt.

As she mused, a melody floated through the garden, soft and compelling, as if the very universe had found its voice. Turning, she saw a figure approaching: Samaveda, a young celestial musician, his lyre cradled in his hands. Each note he played seemed to weave threads of creation into harmony.

He bowed low. "Goddess of dawn, what bothers you?"

Ushas sighed, her voice quiet, vulnerable. "I bring light

to the world, yet I stand apart from it. I see joy bloom in others but feel no root of it within myself."

Samaveda's gaze was gentle. "Perhaps the joy you seek is not absent but misplaced. Light grows brightest when shared. Connection, not solitude, is the seed of vitality."

His words lingered like a melody yet unfinished, stirring something within her. That evening, Ushas made a decision. Summoning her strength, she invited gods, mortals, and celestial beings to a grand festival in Amaravati.

On the day of the festival she declared, "Tonight, we celebrate not the dawn but the bonds that unite us."

The garden came alive with music and laughter as dusk fell. The air hummed with vitality, the streams reflecting the glow of celestial lights. Ushas, usually a distant figure in her radiance, stepped into the celebration—not as a goddess, but as a participant.

She danced with mortals under starlit skies, her movements unburdened by divine expectation. She sang with celestial musicians, their harmonies weaving stories of shared existence. She listened to the laughter of sages, their mirth a balm to her soul. With every moment, she felt her light refracted through the joy of others, returning to her in a warmth she had never known.

Drawn by the familiar strains of Samaveda's music, Ushas found him amidst the celebration. His notes carried the depth of connection, each one resonating like a heartbeat. "Your songs hold a power I cannot name," she said, her voice softened by awe. "What is their secret?"

Samaveda smiled, his gaze steady. "Joy is not born in isolation. Every note I play arises from the world around me—the people, the connections, the shared stories. It is in togetherness that we find the essence of life."

As the festival reached its zenith, Samaveda presented Ushas with a single golden flower. "This blooms only at the height of shared celebration," he said. "It carries the essence of connection and joy."

Moved beyond words, Ushas planted the flower at the center of Amaravati. From it grew a radiant tree, its golden blossoms filling the air with a fragrance that seemed to hold the festival's laughter, music, and love. The tree became a symbol of what Ushas had discovered: that vitality is not solitary. It is found in the bonds we nurture, the moments we share, and the lives we touch.

From that day forward, every dawn she brought, carried the memory of that night. Each golden ray of sunlight was a reminder—not just of beauty, but of connection. Ushas was no longer alone in her radiance. Her light became a bridge, uniting the world in a celebration of existence.

Moral of the Story

True joy is found in connection and shared experiences. Celebrating relationships and embracing the bonds that unite us allow our light to shine brighter and our lives to feel richer.

Modern-Day Relevance

In today's fast-paced, individualistic world, it's easy to

overlook the importance of relationships and shared joy. Ushas's story reminds us that:

> In Friendships and Relationships: Many people today feel disconnected despite being surrounded by others, much like Ushas before the festival. The story reminds us to nurture meaningful connections, whether through sharing meals, having heartfelt conversations, or celebrating milestones together.
>
> In Celebrating Life's Moments: From weddings to birthdays to everyday victories, life offers countless reasons to come together. By celebrating these moments with others, we amplify our joy, just as Ushas found deeper fulfillment in the shared joy of Amaravati's festival.
>
> In Workplaces or Communities: A collaborative project thrives when people contribute their unique strengths while celebrating their shared purpose. Recognizing and valuing these connections can lead to greater fulfillment and a sense of belonging.

Purva Phalguni's energy calls us to revel in the beauty of life and the bonds that make it meaningful, reminding us that love and connection are at the heart of vitality.

Real-Life Analogies for the New Seekers

> Analogy 1: A Potluck Dinner
>
> Imagine hosting a potluck dinner where everyone brings a dish to share. The gathering isn't about the individual dishes themselves but about the warmth, laughter, and connection created as

people come together to share their food, stories, and presence.

Takeaway: Like Ushas realizing her light was amplified by sharing it, the joy of a potluck comes from the collective energy and connection of the group.

Analogy 2: A Band's Harmony

Think of a band where each musician plays their instrument with skill. While each performance is meaningful, the true magic happens when they play together, creating a harmony that none of them could achieve alone.

Takeaway: Like Samaveda's music, which resonated because it came from connection, our joy deepens when it's shared, just as a melody gains richness when multiple notes blend.

Ushas's story teaches us that joy is not a solitary pursuit but a shared experience. Whether it's through friendships, family, or community, the light of our lives shines brightest when it illuminates others. Celebrate the connections that enrich your life, for they are the true essence of vitality and purpose.

It is also important to note how Purva Phalguni's energy fosters not just physical procreation, as often misunderstood, but the creation of meaningful bonds, artistic expressions, and the celebration of life's beauty through joy and togetherness. It encourages seeing relationships and creativity as divine acts that honor the gift of life.

Practical Exercises for the Lunar Mansion

1. Visualization: The Grove of Joy

Close your eyes and imagine yourself in a sunlit grove filled with vibrant flowers, soft grass, and the gentle laughter of loved ones. Picture yourself surrounded by people you cherish, sharing moments of connection, joy, and celebration. Let the warmth and love of the grove fill your heart with vitality and gratitude.

2. Journaling Prompt

Reflect on the relationships that bring joy and vitality to your life.

> Who are the people that uplift you, and why?
>
> How can you strengthen these connections and celebrate them more often?

Write about a moment when you truly celebrated life—what made it memorable, and how can you create more such moments?

3. Action for the Day

Plan a small celebration or gathering with loved ones. Whether it's a meal, a call, or simply sharing kind or grateful words, let this act of connection and joy honor Purva Phalguni's vibrant energy.

Advanced Exercises to Harness the Energy of Purva Phalguni

a) Meditation with Sound

Purpose: Align with Purva Phalguni's energy of love and celebration.

Meditate for 15 minutes to harp melodies interwoven with cascading water droplets. Feel joy and vitality energising every aspect of your life.

b) Connect to Nature

Purpose: Embody Purva Phalguni's energy of relaxation and celebration.

Spend time in a flower-filled garden, enjoying the beauty and peace of the natural world. Reflect on how nature effortlessly celebrates life in its cycles of bloom and rest.

c) Perform a Service

Purpose: Spread joy and connection to others.

Perform an act of kindness that celebrates someone's value in your life—write a heartfelt handwritten note, offer a thoughtful gift, or help someone feel appreciated and loved. Do not expect anything in return.

"Life's truest celebration is found in sharing joy; love is the thread that weaves us into wholeness."

LUNAR MANSION 12: UTTARA PHALGUNI

Beneath the steady gaze of **Beta Leonis (Denebola)**, a story unfolds of quiet strength and enduring purpose. Symbolized by the **Back Legs of a Bed** and ruled by the **Sun's** brilliance, Uttara Phalguni guides us to the crossroads where cosmic wisdom meets earthly service. This nakshatra straddles the noble courage of its zodiac signs **Leo** as well as the meticulous grace of **Virgo**, under the guardianship of the **Sun and Mercury** respectively.

At its heart lies a spiritual truth often whispered but rarely heeded: **"True strength lies in supporting others. Responsibility anchors the soul in purpose."** Uttara Phalguni is not merely a celestial body; it is a mentor, urging us to discover the profound power of service—not as an obligation but as a sacred thread binding us to the universe's intricate design.

As we journey through this mansion of light, let us explore how service transcends duty to become the soul's deepest act of self-realization.

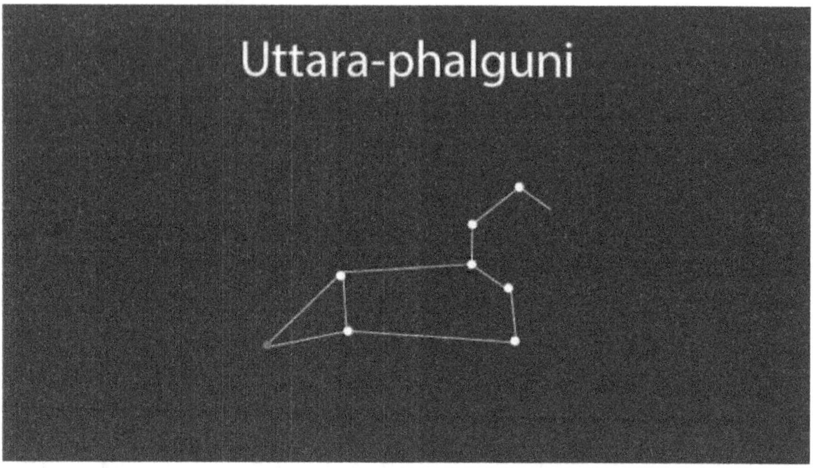

Image Source: https://popularvedicscience.com/ astrology/uttara-phalguni-nakshatra

---

The Tale of Shibi: The King Who Carried the Weight of the World

The Context

Throughout history, leaders and rulers have been celebrated not for their power alone but for their commitment to justice and service. In Indian mythology, the story of King Shibi epitomizes these virtues. Shibi's tale, deeply rooted in the concept of *dharma*[*] (moral order, duty), reveals the essence of leadership as selfless service and the willingness to bear the burdens of others.

This myth-inspired story of Shibi resonates universally as a lesson in responsibility and sacrifice. For spiritual seekers and leaders alike, it serves as a timeless reminder: true strength is measured not by dominance but by compassion and the ability to serve.

The Story

The kingdom of Shibipura was known far and wide for its prosperity. Its rivers sparkled like molten silver, and the fields rolled endlessly in shades of green. At its heart stood King Shibi, a monarch whose name was synonymous with justice. To his people, Shibi was more than a king; he was a protector, a living embodiment of dharma, the cosmic law that binds the world in balance.

Shibi carried his duties with quiet resolve. To him, the strength of the throne was not in power but in responsibility—ensuring that even the weakest had a place under its shelter. His court was a haven, where no plea was too small, and no injustice too trivial.

One morning, as the first light painted the horizon gold, Shibi's court was disrupted by a sudden commotion. A dove, its feathers streaked with dirt and fear, burst into the hall. It fluttered wildly before landing at the king's feet.

"Protect me, O King," it pleaded, its voice trembling. "A hawk pursues me. I have nowhere else to go."

Shibi bent low, his gaze meeting the dove's frightened eyes. Before he could reply, a hawk swooped into the hall, its presence a sharp contrast to the dove's fragility. It perched before the throne, its eyes unwavering.

"That dove is mine," the hawk said, its tone calm yet firm. "It is nature's way. Without it, I cannot survive. If you deny me my prey, you disrupt the balance of life itself."

Shibi stood, his expression thoughtful. "It is indeed the way of nature for the strong to sustain themselves through the weak. But it is also the duty of the strong to protect those who seek refuge. I cannot let harm come to one who trusts me to shield them."

The hawk's head tilted, its voice laced with cunning. "Your words are noble, King, but words alone do not sustain life. If you will protect this dove, you must offer me an equal weight of flesh in return. Such is the cost of fairness."

The court fell silent. Shibi did not flinch. "If that is what must be done, I accept."

A scale was brought to the hall, its chains clanking as it was set before the throne. Shibi placed the trembling dove on one side and took a blade in his hand. Without hesitation, he cut a portion of flesh from his arm and placed it on the scale. Blood darkened his robe, but the dove's weight remained heavier.

"Not enough," the hawk said, its tone unyielding. "The balance remains unmet."

Shibi did not falter. Again and again, he cut, the blade biting deeper each time. His blood pooled at his feet, and whispers of concern rippled through the court. The ministers, the guards, even the common folk begged him to stop. But Shibi, though pale and trembling, remained resolute.

Finally, he placed the blade aside. "If my flesh alone cannot meet the weight of this responsibility, then I offer my entire self." He stepped onto the scale, his body weak but his spirit unbroken.

As his full weight settled on the scale, a brilliant light erupted in the hall, bathing the space in golden hues. Gasps filled the air as the dove and the hawk transformed, their shapes shifting into the divine forms of Indra, king of the gods, and Agni, the god of fire. Their divine presence filled the court with awe.

"You have proven the essence of true strength," Indra said, his voice resonant and warm. "Strength is not in dominion but in the willingness to bear the weight of others' burdens."

Agni stepped forward, his gaze steady. "Your act of selfless service has restored balance across your kingdom. You are *dharma* personified, King Shibi."

As the gods raised their hands in blessing, Shibi's wounds closed, and his strength returned. The blood that had stained the floor shimmered and vanished, as if the earth itself honored his sacrifice.

The court erupted in praise, yet Shibi remained humble. The gods' words echoed in his heart, anchoring him further in his purpose: strength without service is hollow, but responsibility gives life its meaning.

Years later, in a village square of Shibipura, a traveler paused before a simple statue. It depicted King Shibi seated on a scale, his expression serene, the dove and the hawk by his side. When the traveler asked a villager about its significance, they smiled and said:

"This is King Shibi, who taught us that true strength is found in serving others. His legacy isn't just in this statue

—it lives in how we care for one another, as he cared for us."

And in that quiet moment, the traveler saw that the heart of the kingdom's prosperity was not its wealth, but the enduring strength of shared purpose in the minds of its people.

Moral of the Story

True leadership is not about power or privilege—it is about service. Responsibility is not a burden to be avoided but a purpose to be embraced, for it is through supporting others that we find our greatest strength.

Modern-Day Relevance

In today's world, where individualism often takes precedence, Shibi's story reminds us of the power of selfless service and shared responsibility:

> Leadership in the Workplace: A manager who supports their team by taking responsibility during challenging times exemplifies Shibi's spirit. Instead of shifting blame or avoiding accountability, they lead by example, fostering trust and unity.
>
> Lesson from Shibi: True leadership requires bearing the weight of others' challenges and creating an environment of fairness and support.
>
> Community Service: Volunteering for a cause—whether feeding the homeless, mentoring youth, or protecting the environment—reflects the principle that service brings fulfillment. By taking on responsibility for the greater good, we strengthen

the fabric of our communities.

Lesson from Shibi: The act of serving others not only helps those in need but also gives deeper purpose to our own lives.

Personal Relationships: Supporting a loved one through illness, grief, or hardship is an act of service that requires strength, patience, and selflessness. Such responsibility may feel burdensome but often strengthens bonds and provides emotional growth.

Lesson from Shibi: Taking responsibility for others' well-being can be challenging, but it deepens our connections and enriches our lives.

Uttara Phalguni's energy calls us to see responsibility not as a weight to be carried but as a purpose that anchors us, connecting us to the greater flow of life. Through service, we discover our truest strength.

Real-Life Analogies for the New Seekers

1. A Mother's Sacrifice:

Imagine a mother who works tirelessly to take care of her children. Despite personal hardships and often professional sacrifices, she prioritizes her children's needs, ensuring they have opportunities for growth and happiness. The mother's strength is not in physical might but in her unwavering commitment to her responsibility, which gives her life purpose and direction.

Key Takeaway: Like King Shibi offering himself for

the dove, selfless actions rooted in responsibility create harmony and nurture those who depend on us.

Note: This example is not intended to be gender biased in any way or to undermine the role of the father. Rather, it is a tribute to mothers in several parts of the world where they sacrifice disproportionately for their family.

---

2. A Teacher's Devotion:

Consider a dedicated teacher in an underserved community. Despite limited resources, the teacher pours their energy into educating children, helping them overcome barriers to success. Their work is challenging, but the knowledge that they are shaping lives gives them the strength to persist. Such selfless teachers really do exist all over the world.

Key Takeaway: Just as Shibi balanced the scales with his sacrifice, the teacher's commitment restores balance and opportunity to those in need.

Practical Exercises for the Lunar Mansion

1. Visualization: The Pillar of Support

Close your eyes and imagine yourself as a tall, sturdy pillar supporting a grand structure. Around you are people relying on your strength, yet you also feel connected to an infinite source of energy that sustains you. Visualize your support creating harmony and balance in the lives of others while anchoring your own sense of purpose.

2. Journaling Prompt

Reflect on the responsibilities you carry in your life.

> How do these roles give your life meaning and purpose?
>
> Are there ways you can balance your own needs while serving others?

Write about a time when supporting someone brought you a sense of fulfillment. How can you continue to offer strength without feeling overwhelmed?

3. Action for the Day

Take on an act of responsibility that benefits someone else. Whether it's helping a colleague, supporting a family member, or volunteering your time, let this act remind you of the strength that comes from serving others. If possible, make a commitment to repeat this act.

Advanced Exercises to Harness the Energy of Uttara Phalguni

a) Meditation with Sound

> Purpose: Align with Uttara Phalguni's energy of service and responsibility.
>
> Meditate for 15 minutes to low, steady temple gongs. Let the vibrations anchor you in

responsibility and inspire purposeful action.

b) Connect to Nature

Purpose: Embody Uttara Phalguni's grounding and supportive energy.

Spend time near a mountain or a large boulder which is providing support to trees,shrubs,animals,insects,etc. Reflect on its unyielding presence and stability, symbolizing the strength you offer to those who rely on you.

c) Perform a Service

Purpose: Strengthen your connection to Uttara Phalguni's energy by supporting others.

Offer your time or resources to someone who could benefit from your support—mentor a junior colleague, assist a neighbor, or volunteer for a cause. Let your actions reflect the power of responsibility anchored in compassion. Do not expect anything in return.

"Responsibility is the anchor that keeps the soul steady amidst life's storms."

LUNAR MANSION 13: HASTA

Hasta gleams in the night sky as a reminder of human potential. This mansion, formed by the stars **Delta, Gamma, Epsilon, Alpha, and Beta Corvi (Corvus)**, paints a picture of dexterity and precision. Its symbol, the **Hand**, speaks of skill, creation, and the power to shape the world —a reflection of its planetary Lord, **the Moon**, which governs the tides of emotion and inspiration.

Anchored within the **Virgo** (ruled by **Mercury)** zodiac, Hasta merges the analytical brilliance of Mercury with the nurturing rhythm of its own planetary ruler Moon. Together, they whisper an ancient truth: the act of creating is not just a skill but a sacred journey.

The spiritual theme of Hasta, **Skill and Manifestation**, encourages you to align intention with action. As the Cosmic message proclaims, **"Your hands shape your destiny. Work with intention to create a meaningful life."** This mansion urges you to recognize the divine tools at your disposal—not just your hands, but your mind, heart, and will.

As we step into the domain of Hasta, let us explore its wisdom, not as an abstract philosophy, but as a living energy waiting to flow through us. Each deliberate act, each crafted effort, is a prayer to the universe—a testament to our ability to manifest dreams into reality.

Image Source: https://popularvedicscience.com/astrology/hasta-nakshatra

---

The Tale of the Radiant Artisan

Context for Readers

As per Vedic Astrology, each of the 27 Nakshatras, or lunar mansions, represents unique energies and lessons, guiding humanity toward spiritual growth and personal mastery. Hasta, the 13th Nakshatra, is symbolized by an open hand—a representation of craftsmanship, skill, and the ability to manifest intentions into reality.

This story is based in the land of the Sun God (Surya), whose radiance empowers creation, clarity, and focus. The myth inspired story of Hasta beautifully illustrates how skillful action, guided by intention, can shape one's destiny and inspire others.

The Story

In the radiant halls of Surya Loka, where the Sun God presided over endless light and boundless possibility, there lived a young celestial artisan named Arka. His hands were legendary, crafting wonders that left even the gods in awe—delicate patterns carved into unyielding diamonds, molten gold shaped into forms so lifelike they seemed ready to spring into motion. Yet, despite his renown, Arka had a sense of void deep within, an unspoken yearning that even his most flawless creations could not satisfy.

One day, Surya, the Sun God, found him in his workshop, surrounded by unfinished pieces, his usually steady hands hesitating over his tools.

"What troubles you, Arka?" Surya asked, his voice as warm as dawn.

Arka set his tools down and sighed. "I create endlessly, yet it feels hollow. My hands are skilled, but my work lacks meaning. I want to craft something that reflects your brilliance, something that truly matters."

Surya's gaze softened. "Skill without purpose is like sunlight scattered in a storm—seen but unfocused. Come, let me show you how hands, guided by intention, can shape more than objects—they can shape destinies."

Surya brought Arka to Earth, where they arrived in a village steeped in quiet despair. The fields were cracked and lifeless, and the people, though hardworking, bore the weight of constant failure. Among them was an old potter, his hands calloused and cracked as he shaped clay on a warped wheel. His pots crumbled after a single use, and the villagers, disillusioned, had stopped seeking his wares. Still, the potter toiled in solitude, his eyes dim with the shadow of futility.

"Help him," Surya instructed, pointing toward the potter. "Not with divine brilliance, but with the wisdom of your hands."

Arka hesitated. He was used to creating grand wonders, not aiding mortals in mundane struggles. Yet, he approached the potter, his voice humble. "May I assist you?"

The potter glanced up, his face lined with years of disappointment. With a slow nod, he stepped aside, offering his seat to Arka.

Arka sat and studied the potter's tools, realizing their imperfections. His hands moved instinctively, shaping a new wheel from the clay of the earth, its form simple yet precise. He infused it with the warmth of his touch, creating a tool not of grandeur but of function. "Try this," Arka said, offering it to the potter. "And trust your hands."

The potter placed a lump of clay on the new wheel and began to spin. The transformation was subtle at first—a smoother turn, a steadier rhythm—but soon, the pots began to take shape. These pots were now strong, elegant, and enduring. They enabled the villagers to carry water to thirsty fields and food to hungry mouths. As the villagers saw the change, they returned, their faith in the potter was restored. Their smiles were radiant, their gratitude overflowing, and in their joy, something within Arka transformed.

For the first time, he saw his hands not as tools of creation for creation's sake, but as instruments capable of lifting others, of shaping lives. His restlessness subsided, replaced by a quiet certainty.

When Arka returned to Surya Loka, Surya awaited him, holding a radiant bracelet forged from pure sunlight. “This is yours,” the Sun God said, fastening it around Arka’s wrist. “But it’s true value will only be revealed when your heart understands its purpose.”

Arka wore the bracelet with pride, believing it would enhance his already legendary skill. But as he worked, he noticed something strange—his creations, though intricate and beautiful, felt lifeless. The light of the bracelet seemed to overshadow his efforts, dulling their impact. Frustrated, Arka cast it aside and returned to Earth, seeking clarity.

Back in the village, he wandered aimlessly until he saw a child laughing, chasing sunlight reflected off a pot the old potter had made. The child’s joy was unrestrained, pure, and it struck a chord deep within Arka. This simple pot, shaped with care and purpose, had brought life to this moment in the child’s life.

It was not the bracelet or even his skill that truly mattered—it was the intention behind his work. In serving the potter and, through him, the village, Arka had created something far greater than beauty: he had created meaning.

When Arka returned to Surya Loka, the bracelet shimmered once more, its light no longer external but a reflection of his own.

Surya smiled, his voice steady and knowing. “Now you understand. Your hands shape not just objects but the world around you. Guided by purpose, they create enduring utility, not merely things."

Arka bowed, his heart alight with a newfound clarity. From that day, his work was no longer driven by the need for perfection but by the quiet resolve to make a difference. Each creation became a story, each movement of his hands a step toward shaping a meaningful life.

Moral of the Story

Skill without intention is hollow. Mastery lies not in the beauty of creation alone, but in the purpose it serves. When our hands work with intention, they shape not only objects but also the lives they touch.

Modern-Day Relevance

In our modern lives, we often get caught up in pursuing accolades, wealth, or perfection, forgetting the deeper purpose behind our work. Arka's story reminds us to:

> Professionally: An artist who paints merely for fame may feel unfulfilled. But when their art expresses a message or brings joy to others, it becomes meaningful.
>
> Personally: A person might spend hours perfecting a social media post to garner likes, but if they instead use that time to share something authentic or helpful, they contribute to a positive, inspiring narrative for others.
>
> Spiritually: Recognize that our skills and talents are gifts meant to contribute to a greater good.

Arka's story resonates deeply in today's fast-paced world. It reminds us to align our actions with our values, ensuring that what we create is not just beautiful but also meaningful. Hasta's energy encourages us to be both skilled and intentional, shaping our destiny with purpose.

Real-Life Analogies for the New Seekers

1. Crafting a Masterpiece with Purpose:

Imagine an artist painting a mural. If the artist focuses solely on impressing others, their work may lack depth and authenticity. However, if the artist paints with the intention to inspire or communicate a message, the mural becomes more than just a picture—it becomes a transformative experience for both the creator and the viewer.

Key Takeaway: Purpose infuses skill with meaning, turning work into a soulful expression.

2. Building a Community Project:

Consider a skilled architect building a community center. If the focus is only on grandiose designs to attract attention, the project might overlook practical needs. However, if the architect designs with the community and functionality in mind—adding accessible features and spaces for learning—the center becomes a hub of unity and growth.

Key Takeaway: True fulfillment lies in creating something that nurtures and uplifts others.

Practical Exercises for the Lunar Mansion

1. Visualization: The Hands of Creation

Close your eyes and imagine your hands glowing with radiant energy, capable of shaping and manifesting anything you desire. Visualize yourself crafting something meaningful —a sculpture, a home, or even a better version of yourself. Feel the joy and satisfaction of seeing your intentions take tangible form through your efforts.

2. Journaling Prompt

Reflect on how your hands have shaped your life so far.

What are the things you've created or achieved with your skills and effort?

How can you use your abilities to manifest your dreams?

Write about a project or goal you've been meaning to start. What's the first step you can take to bring it to life?

3. Action for the Day

Create something with your hands today—a meal, a paper boat, a piece of art, or even an organized space. Focus on the act of creating as a mindful expression of your intentions and talents.

Advanced Exercises to Harness the Energy of Hasta

a) Meditation with Sound

Purpose: Align with Hasta's energy of manifestation and skill.

Meditate for 15 minutes to rhythmic hand claps paired with snapping fingers. Imagine the beats shaping your intentions into tangible creations.

b) Connect to Nature

Purpose: Embody Hasta's creative and tactile energy.

Spend time gardening, planting seeds, or simply feeling the texture of soil, leaves, or tree bark. Let the connection to nature inspire your creativity and remind you of the harmony between intention and action.

c) Perform a Service

Purpose: Use your skills to help others.

Offer your expertise or create something to assist someone—a meal for a friend, a repair for a neighbor, or a tool for a colleague. Let your hands channel the energy of service and creativity. Do not expect anything in return.

"Your hands are architects of destiny; shape the world with intention and the heart will follow."

LUNAR MANSION 14: CHITRA

In the vast expanse of the celestial canvas, **Chitra** emerges as a radiant gem, its light piercing through the cosmos like a beacon of **creative beauty** and **illumination.** Its astronomical identity, **Spica** (Alpha Virginis), anchors it as one of the most brilliant stars, a jewel not just in the night sky but in the zodiac's symphony of energy. Governed by **Mars**, symbolized by a **bright jewel or pearl**, this nakshatra invites us to uncover the treasures hidden within ourselves.

As it bridges the dual zodiacs of **Virgo** and **Libra**, under the stewardship of **Mercury** and **Venus** respectively, Chitra whispers a timeless truth: that **beauty is a reflection of inner truth**, a mirror to the essence we embody. To honor Chitra is to align with this cosmic message: **"Illuminate the world by aligning with your essence."**

In this chapter, we dive into the brilliance of Chitra, exploring how it transforms raw potential into refined splendor, much like the cosmos polishing its own jewel. Let us journey together into its radiance.

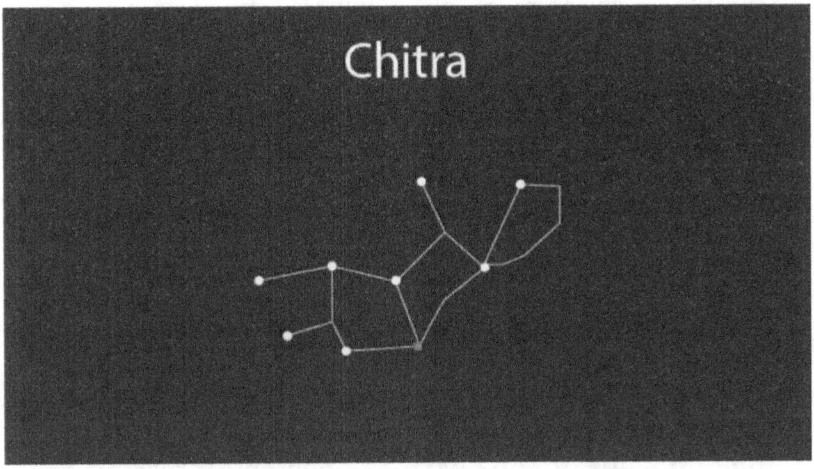

Image Source: https://popularvedicscience.com/astrology/chitra-nakshatra

---

The Tale of *Vishwakarma and the Jewel of Illumination**

Context for readers

In Indian mythology, Vishwakarma is revered as the celestial architect of the universe. His creations—divine palaces, celestial weapons, and extraordinary structures—are unparalleled in beauty and craftsmanship. This myth-inspired story weaves Vishwakarma's quest to create not just flawless forms but works that reflect the essence of inner truth, aligning perfectly with Chitra's cosmic message.

The Story

Vishwakarma, the divine architect of the universe, stood before his latest creation: a palace so radiant that its walls seemed to hum with the light of a thousand stars. The gods would marvel, he knew, but as he gazed at his masterpiece, any sense of joy or pride failed to enter his heart. The brilliance of his work felt inadequate, as if it lacked a breath, a heartbeat.

"It is flawless," he thought, running his hand along a shimmering wall. "Then why does it feel incomplete?"

Word of the palace spread quickly, and soon the gods gathered to witness its splendor. Among them was *Narada**, the wise and mischievous sage, his gaze sharp as he studied the palace.

"Magnificent," Narada said, his voice like a note in a melody. "But Vishwakarma, does this creation truly reflect you?"

Vishwakarma frowned. "What do you mean?"

"Beauty," Narada replied, "is not found in perfection alone. True beauty is a reflection of the creator's essence, even if it means showing their vulnerabilities. Does this palace reveal your truths?"

The words lodged in Vishwakarma's heart like an unstruck chord. He had built countless marvels, each more intricate than the last. Yet now, faced with Narada's question, doubt flickered. "How can I create something that reveals my truth?"

Narada's smile was gentle. "Seek the Jewel of Illumination. It lies deep within the heart of the asteroid cloud. Only its light can show you how to unite form and essence." Vishwakarma hesitated, but the longing to fill the void within him outweighed his pride. He left his tools and creations behind, stepping into the unknown.

The asteroid cloud greeted him like an ancient guardian, sharp rocks flying all over at great speeds, their shadows and dust whispering like old storytellers. The air was thick with an unfamiliar scent and unseen mysteries. As he ventured deeper, doubts began to stir, slipping into his mind like the strange clouds of mist curling around his feet.

"Your creations are already perfect," the rocks hissed. "Why seek more? Why risk failure?"

Vishwakarma paused, the intensity of their words pressing against him. But a flicker of determination lit within—a yearning to uncover what perfection alone could not satisfy. He pressed on.

The asteroid cloud transformed into a labyrinth of illusions. Pathways looped endlessly, mountains shifted as though alive, and the stars above seemed to mock his search. Days bled into weeks, and despair began to claw at him. Yet just when his spirit wavered, he stumbled upon a crater that glowed faintly in the darkness. At its center lay the Jewel of Illumination, a gem pulsing with light that seemed to breathe.

As Vishwakarma reached for it, a voice resonated from the crater, deep and resonant. "Why do you seek me, craftsman?"

"To bring truth to my creations," Vishwakarma replied, his voice steady despite the weariness in his body.

The light of the jewel flared, surrounding him in brilliance. "Then you must first face yourself," the voice said.

Memories flashed in Vishwakarma's mind, unrelenting as the jewel's light enveloped him. He saw his triumphs —palaces, temples, bridges—all impeccable, yet each one distant, untouched by his heart. He saw the moments when doubt had crept in, the times he had silenced his inner voice in the pursuit of perfection.

The voice spoke again. "You create for others, but do you honor the beauty within yourself?"

The question untangled something deep within him. He realized that his creations, though dazzling, lacked his essence. They reflected his skill in achieving perfection, but not his truths, neither his vulnerability, nor his soul. Perfection had been his goal, but it was not what his spirit yearned for.

When Vishwakarma emerged from the asteroid cloud, the Jewel of Illumination glowed softly in his hand. Back in his workshop, he did not reach for his tools immediately. Instead, he sat in quiet reflection, allowing the light of the jewel to guide him.

This time, when he began to create, his hands moved with a different rhythm. He poured not just his precision but his soul into the work. What emerged was the Radiant Veil, a structure that defied expectations. Its form was simple, but its surface shimmered with a living light. The Veil looked ordinary at first glance, it did not dazzle with its design—but it transformed those who gazed upon it.

The gods gathered again to see his latest creation, silent as they stood before the Veil. Each saw their reflection, not as they appeared, but as they truly were. Their fears, their joys, their unspoken desires shimmered in the light, undeniable yet beautiful.

Narada stepped forward, awe softening his mischievous gaze. “This is your greatest creation, Vishwakarma,” he said. “It does not merely please the eye. It illuminates the truth.”

Vishwakarma smiled, a quiet peace engulfing him. “The Veil reflects not me but the light within each of us.”

Years later, fragments of the Radiant Veil found their way to Earth. Mortals who gazed into them saw their innermost selves. Some were comforted, finding beauty they had never recognized. Others turned away, unable to confront what lay within. Yet the fragments remained, whispering their eternal truth: “Beauty is a reflection of inner truth. Illuminate the world by aligning with your essence.”

Moral of the Story

True beauty is not in flawless appearances but in reflecting one’s inner truth. When our efforts align with our core essence, our creations and actions radiate a light that inspires and transforms others.

> Creativity and authenticity are inseparable: Like Vishwakarma’s creations, true beauty emerges when skill is combined with the courage to reveal one’s inner essence.
>
> Illuminate the world by aligning with your truth: Whether in art, relationships, or personal growth,

authenticity connects us more deeply with others and ourselves.

Modern-Day Relevance

In a world obsessed with external validation—social media likes, curated personas, and material achievements—Vishwakarma's story serves as a reminder to focus on authenticity and inner truth.

Professionally: Success is not just about delivering perfect results; it's about infusing work with purpose and authenticity.

Personally: Many people put on a facade to gain approval or avoid vulnerability. The Radiant Veil teaches that lasting connections are built when we embrace and reflect our true selves.

In Creative pursuits: Writers, artists, and musicians often struggle between creating what they think will sell and what feels true to them. Vishwakarma's story reminds us that the most resonant creations come from the heart, not just the hand.

In Everyday Choices: Whether it's decorating a home, dressing for the day, or speaking your mind, let your choices reflect your inner truth rather than societal expectations.

By aligning with your essence, you illuminate your life and inspire others to do the same. This is the timeless lesson of Chitra and the Jewel of Illumination.

Real-Life Analogies for New Seekers

1. An Artist Finding Their Voice:

Scenario: A painter spends years perfecting their technique, creating works admired for their technical brilliance but feeling dissatisfied. One day, they decide to paint something deeply personal—a childhood memory, a moment of vulnerability. This painting, though less polished, resonates with viewers in ways their earlier works never did.

Key Lesson: True beauty and impact arise when we allow our creations to reflect our authentic selves rather than striving solely for external perfection.

2. A Job Interview with Honesty:

Scenario: A professional preparing for a job interview rehearses all the "right" answers, presenting a flawless but generic persona. Midway through, they decide to speak candidly about their true motivations and aspirations. Though risky, this vulnerability resonates with the interviewer, leading to a deeper connection and ultimately, the job offer.

Key Lesson: Success and fulfillment often come not from presenting a polished facade but from showing your genuine self.

Practical Exercises for the Lunar Mansion

1. Visualization: The Jewel Within

Close your eyes and imagine yourself as a sculptor chiseling away at a rough block of stone. With each stroke, you uncover a dazzling jewel hidden inside —a radiant reflection of your inner truth. Visualize this jewel glowing brighter with every moment, illuminating the beauty and authenticity within you.

2. Journaling Prompt

Reflect on the unique qualities or talents that make you shine.

> What do you consider your greatest inner treasures?
>
> How can you express these qualities more boldly in your life?

Write about a time when your inner value or beauty inspired others. What did you learn from that experience?

3. Action for the Day

Beautify something in your life today—a room, your workspace, or even your personal appearance. Focus on expressing your unique style and creativity, letting this act reflect your inner essence. You need not do this in a way that the world expects, but do it the way you want to.

Advanced Exercises to Harness the Energy of Chitra

a) Meditation with Sound

Purpose: Connect with Chitra's energy of beauty and illumination.

Meditate for 15 minutes to soft violin strings layered with faint metallic resonance. Picture these sounds illuminating your inner beauty and truth.

b) Connect to Nature

Purpose: Embrace Chitra's creative and radiant energy.

Spend time near natural gemstones, rocks, or crystals. Observe their unique patterns and colors, and let the unique beauty of each of them inspire a deeper appreciation for the uniqueness within yourself.

c) Perform a Service

Purpose: Illuminate someone else's path with beauty or wisdom.

Help someone recognize their own value and beauty. This could be through a compliment, creating something meaningful for them, or simply listening to their story and reflecting back their strengths. Do not expect anything in return.

"Beauty is the light of inner truth reflected in form; illuminate your inner being, and your creations will make the world glow."

LUNAR MANSION 15: SWATI

Beneath the expanse of the dark cosmic shroud, there exists a solitary diamond that whispers of boundless possibility—**Arcturus (Alpha Bootis)**. Swati, with its delicate symbol of **a plant shoot** or **a single blade of grass**, appears fragile but carries the indomitable spirit of **Rahu (the North Node).** Swati invites us to sway without breaking, and to find strength in adaptability. It carries a spiritual theme of **freedom and independence**, offering the cosmic message: **"Flow like the wind—free, adaptable, and open to life's endless possibilities."**

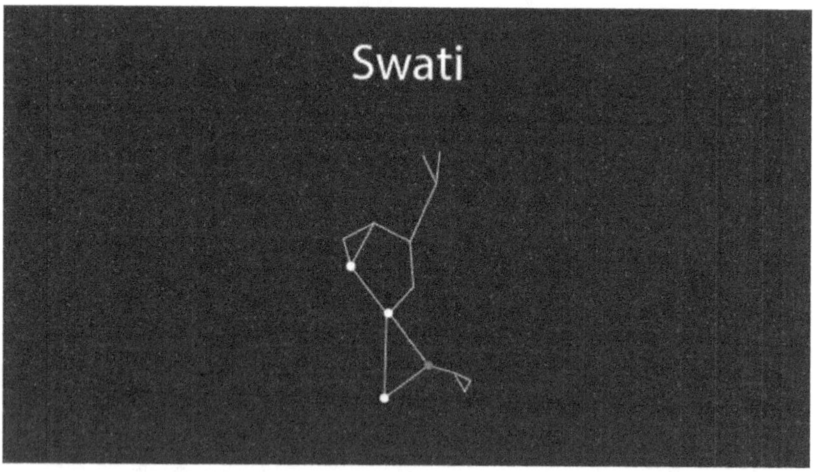

Image Source: https://popularvedicscience.com/astrology/swati-nakshatra

---

The Tale of Vayu and Vaidehi: Freedom in the Wind

Context for Readers

In Indian mythology, natural elements like the wind,

fire, and water are personified as gods with distinct personalities and roles. Vayu, the god of wind, represents freedom, adaptability, and the power of movement. He symbolizes the invisible force that can transform landscapes and lives. In This myth-inspired story, Vayu encounters the Nakshatra (lunar mansion) Swati, which reflects the qualities of the wind: flexibility, independence, and the ability to guide change.

This tale of Vayu and Vaidehi explores the profound nature of freedom—not as a chaotic force but as one that harmonizes and empowers. For readers unfamiliar with Indian mythology, it provides a universal lesson on the balance between independence and responsibility.

The Story

The sky stretched wide and boundless, the perfect stage for Vayu, the God of Winds, to roam. He darted between mountain peaks and vast oceans, playing with clouds, stirring leaves, and carrying whispers across the world. Yet, for all his freedom, he felt restless, like a melody missing its harmony. His currents moved unrestrained, but his heart felt aimless.

Seeking clarity, Vayu turned to Brahma, the Creator. "Why do I feel unfulfilled despite all my freedom?" he asked, his voice shadowed by something unknown. "I traverse worlds and touch everything, yet it feels as though I touch nothing."

Brahma's eyes were steady, his tone timeless. "True freedom is not just in the ability to move at will, Vayu. It is in choosing your path and carrying purpose within your flow. Go to Earth and learn this for yourself."

With a nod, Vayu descended to Earth. His currents brushed forests and rivers, villages and fields. One day, he reached the kingdom of Vasati, a land hemmed in by towering walls. The air was heavy here, suffocating in its stillness. The people moved like shadows, their voices subdued, their steps careful. Something was not right.

Curious, Vayu drifted into the palace gardens. There, he found Vaidehi, the young princess, staring at a bird in a golden cage. The bird's wings twitched, but its song was silent. The princess's gaze mirrored the bird's—a mixture of sorrow and quiet defiance.

Vayu swirled gently around her. "Why does the bird not sing?" he asked, his voice a soft breeze.

Vaidehi startled, searching for the source of the voice. "Who speaks?"

"I am Vayu, the wind. Tell me, why does this place feel so stifled?"

Vaidehi's shoulders drooped. "My father, the king, believes freedom is dangerous. He cages the bird to keep it safe, just as he cages the people with his rules. Music, gatherings, even planting trees are forbidden. He thinks control is order."

Vayu's currents stirred, rippling through the leaves of the garden. "Freedom is not chaos—it is the breath of life itself. Why do you not oppose him?"

Her eyes lifted to the sky, her expression resigned. "I am but one voice. How can one voice change the prevailing order?"

Her words lingered with Vayu, like seeds waiting to take root. As he left the garden, a thought began to form. Over the next few days, he swept through the kingdom, his presence growing stronger. He rattled the iron gates, sent leaves spiraling into the markets, and even toppled a section of the outer wall. The people, at first frightened, began to lift their heads. The breeze carried something they had forgotten—movement, possibility.

The king, enraged, ordered barriers erected and priests summoned to subdue the wind. But Vayu was unyielding, flowing where he pleased, carrying whispers of change. At last, Vaidehi stepped forward.

"Let me speak to the wind," she said. "It seeks not to destroy but to awaken."

In the palace courtyard, Vayu swirled around her, his presence now a gentle caress. "Why do you stand before me?" he asked. "Do you wish to stop me?"

Vaidehi's voice was steady. "I do not wish to stop you. But your force frightens the people. They have forgotten how to breathe freely. Show them that freedom is not a storm, but a breeze that carries growth."

Vayu paused. Her words were like a still pond, reflecting something within himself. "Very well," he said. "I will flow with purpose."

The next day, Vayu returned, no longer a tempest but a guiding wind. He carried the scent of jasmine from the hills, scattered seeds into barren soil, and lifted the villagers' songs into the open air. The people saw the wind changing things all around them. If anyone were to question them for any of these, they could blame the wind. Some of the daring , free spirited folks began to stir, planting new trees, singing in the streets, and tearing down some of the cages that had confined their lives.

The king, watching from the palace, saw his power slipping. Yet instead of fear, he felt something unexpected—a strange sense of peace. He turned to Vaidehi, standing tall as the wind played with her hair. “What is this freedom you speak of?” he asked.

“It is the air we breathe, Father,” she said softly. “It is the space to grow, not the chaos you fear.”

The king hesitated for a few weeks, but the joy on his people’s faces was undeniable. The tempest had disappeared and was replaced by a newfound energy in the city. Things seemed to be... in order. At last, he decreed that the kingdom’s walls be dismantled, its gates opened wide.

Vayu was deeply satisfied as he saw these events unfold. As he prepared to leave, he returned to Vaidehi in the garden. “You have taught me something profound,” he said. “Freedom is not breaking barriers for its own sake. It is creating a conducive environment for life to thrive.”

Vaidehi smiled, her voice warm. “And you have shown me that even the gentlest wind can carry the seeds of change.”

From that day, the kingdom of Vasati became a land of open skies and boundless possibilities. The caged bird flew high into the heavens, its song carried by Vayu to every corner of the earth. The winds, once feared, now whispered of hope, flowing free as life itself.

Moral of the Story

True freedom is not about chaos or rebellion—it is about finding harmony and creating space for growth. Independence is not just about breaking barriers but about guiding others toward purpose and unity.

Modern-Day Relevance

In today's world, freedom is often misunderstood as the absence of rules or constraints. Vayu's story teaches us that:

> Professionally: In workplaces, micromanagement stifles creativity and growth. Empowering employees to make decisions and take ownership of their work mirrors the energy of Swati—freedom balanced with purpose.
>
> Personally: Relationships thrive when partners respect each other's individuality. For example, allowing a loved one to pursue their passions without judgment fosters a deeper bond, just as Vaidehi's wisdom guided Vayu to channel his power with care.
>
> Socially: Societies grow when they balance individual freedoms with collective responsibility. Laws that nurture creativity, education, and equality create an environment where freedom becomes a tool for progress, much like Vayu's gentle winds inspiring change in the kingdom.

The energy of Swati reminds us that freedom is not just about breaking barriers—it is about creating harmony and purpose. Like the wind, we are meant to flow, adapt, and guide ourselves and others toward growth and transformation.

Real-Life Analogies for the New Seekers

1. Real-Life Analogy: The Role of a Mentor

Imagine a manager in a workplace who believes in empowering their team. Instead of micromanaging, they create an environment where their employees can experiment, innovate, and grow. This freedom leads to personal and professional fulfillment for the employees and greater success for the team.

Key Takeaway: Just as Vayu learned to guide with purpose, true freedom lies in fostering growth and harmony, not controlling others.

---

2. Real-Life Analogy: A Child Learning to Ride a Bike

Consider a parent teaching their child to ride a bicycle. At first, the child wobbles and falls, but the parent doesn't hold the bike forever. They gently let go, allowing the child to find their balance and move forward independently. The freedom to explore and fail becomes the foundation of the child's confidence and skill.

Key Takeaway: Like the parent, we can create spaces for growth by trusting others to navigate their own paths, balancing guidance with independence.

Practical Exercises for the Lunar Mansion

1. Visualization: The Dancing Breeze

Close your eyes and imagine yourself as a gentle breeze, flowing freely through an open meadow. Feel the lightness and adaptability of the wind, moving effortlessly around obstacles and carrying seeds of possibility to fertile ground. As you flow, visualize yourself embracing freedom and independence while remaining connected to the larger whole.

2. Journaling Prompt

Reflect on a time when you felt truly free—emotionally, mentally, or physically.

What contributed to this sense of freedom?

How can you recreate or sustain this feeling in your current life?

Write about an area in your life where you feel constrained. What steps can you take to break free or approach the situation with more flexibility?

3. Action for the Day

Do something spontaneous today—a small adventure, a creative activity, or an unplanned act of kindness. Embrace the energy of freedom and adaptability, and allow it to bring fresh perspective and joy into your day.

Advanced Exercises to Harness the Energy of Swati

a) Meditation with Sound

Purpose: Align with Swati's energy of freedom and independence.

Meditate for 15 minutes to bamboo flute tones carried by light breezes. Feel yourself moving freely like the wind, unbound and adaptable.

b) Connect to Nature

Purpose: Embody Swati's airy and adaptable essence.

Spend time outdoors on a breezy day, feeling the wind against your skin. Reflect on how the wind adapts, flows, and carries energy across vast distances, inspiring you to embrace flexibility and independence.

c) Perform a Service

Purpose: Help someone find or reclaim their sense of freedom.

Offer support to someone feeling stuck—whether it's helping them organize their thoughts, exploring solutions together, or encouraging them to take a leap of faith. Your guidance can help them embrace their own Swati energy. Do not expect anything in return.

"Freedom is the dance of the soul unbound, flowing with life's winds without resistance."

LUNAR MANSION 16: VISHAKHA

Three stars converge like celestial markers: **Alpha Librae (Zubenelgenubi), Beta Librae (Zubeneschamali)**, and **Gamma Librae**. Their timeless glow whispers of Vishakha, a mansion whose symbol, the **Triumphal Arch**, stands tall—a gateway that dares dreamers to embrace purpose. Guided by **Jupiter**, the expansive lord of wisdom, and influenced by the harmonious energy of **Libra** (lord being **Venus)** and the transformative force of **Scorpio (Mars)**, Vishakha is both a challenge and an invitation.

Here, the theme of **focus and determination** unfolds as a cosmic message: **"Focus transforms the scattered into the meaningful. Determination births success."**

Every soul crossing this arch must wrestle with distraction and doubt, for only those with unwavering intent can step through and claim the victories promised by the universe.

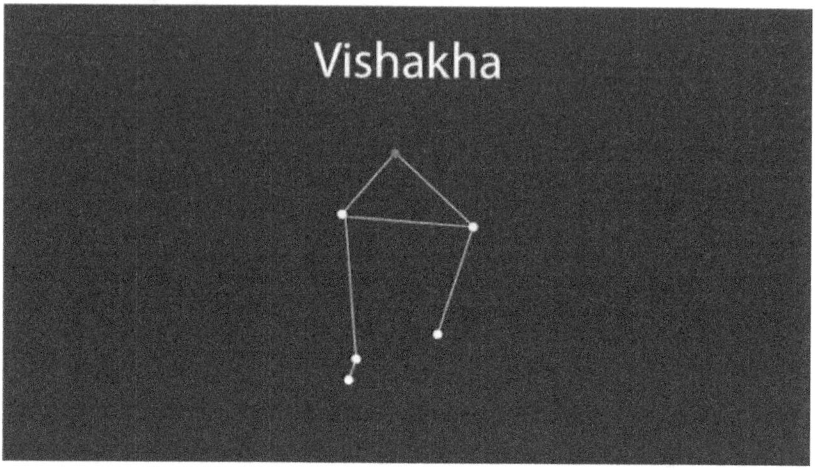

Image Source: https://popularvedicscience.com/astrology/vishakha-nakshatra

The Tale of Vishakha: Indra, Agni, and Quest for the Potion of Joy

---

Context for Readers

In Indian mythology, gods and celestial beings often undertook incredible quests to sustain the balance of the cosmos. These stories are rich with lessons about human nature, resilience, and transformation. One such tale involves Indra, the king of the heavens, and Agni, the god of fire, as they embark on a daring mission to obtain the Potion of Joy. This potion, believed to be the essence of life itself, is guarded by obstacles that demand unyielding focus and determination. Their journey through the Nakshatra of Vishakha reveals the transformative power of perseverance and clarity of purpose.

The Story

The heavens were filled with unease. Indra, ruler of

the heavens, sat depressed on his throne, his once-bright demeanor dimmed by an invisible concern. Across realms, vitality waned—gods and mortals alike faltered, their strength leeched away by a creeping malaise. The sages had spoken, and their revelation was clear: salvation from this trouble lay in the Potion of Joy, hidden within the forest of Vishakha, a place of trials as formidable as the potion's promise. Guarded by illusions, storms, and ancient forces, the forest tested not strength, but resolve.

Indra's voice cut through the uneasy stillness. "I cannot face this alone," he admitted. His gaze turned to Agni, the fire god whose light held the power to pierce shadows. "Will you join me on this quest?"

Agni's flames flickered with a resolve. "Focus will guide us, and determination will carry us. Together, we will not falter."

The forest loomed ahead, a labyrinth of shifting forms and unrelenting whispers. With their first steps into its depths, the air seemed alive, shimmering with mirages of desires crafted to seduce and ensnare.

Indra froze as a vision emerged before him: a throne of stars, radiant and adorned, with every being in the cosmos bowing in adoration. The ache of longing gripped his heart, pulling him toward the image. "What harm lies in dreaming?" he murmured.

Beside him, Agni's flames flared, cutting through the illusion. "Dreams without purpose lead to ruin," he said, his tone steady. "Your throne is nothing but smoke. Stay focused, or we will lose ourselves."

The mirage dissolved, and Indra's cheeks flushed with the sting of truth. Humbled, he stepped back onto the path, letting Agni lead them deeper.

The forest thickened, its stillness shattered by a roaring storm. Winds screamed, lightning raged, and the earth trembled. Indra stepped forward, confident in his command of storms. "This is my domain," he declared. He raised his arms to summon control, but the winds twisted mockingly, tearing through his authority. His power felt scattered, useless against the tempest's ferocity.

"We cannot master it!" Agni's voice rose above the din. "We must endure it!"

Planting their feet against the ground, they leaned into the storm. Agni's flames cut through the biting cold, creating pockets of warmth, while Indra's unyielding strength anchored them. The storm roared in defiance, but they stood firm, letting its fury crash against them. Slowly, as if recognizing their determination, the winds stilled, and the forest quieted once more.

At the heart of the forest lay the chalice bearing the potion of Joy, shimmering golden and pure, cradled within the coils of a massive serpent. Its eyes glowed with ancient wisdom, its voice a hiss that resonated through the clearing.

"Why do you seek this potion?" the serpent demanded. "Do you think it will grant you power, glory, or peace? Only those with true purpose may pass."

Indra stepped forward, his voice measured and steady. “We do not seek it for ourselves, but for the balance of existence. Without it, life falters.”

The serpent’s gaze shifted to Agni. “And you, fire god? What drives you to this pursuit?”

Agni’s flames dimmed to a steady glow. “My nature is to burn away falsehood and illuminate truth. We seek the potion not for conquest, but for renewal.”

The serpent stared, unmoving. It took its own time to get convinced, before its coils loosened. Eventually, it withdrew, revealing the chalice. Indra approached and bowed, before lifting it carefully. The potion inside the chalice was glowing like captured sunlight.

As they turned to leave, the serpent spoke once more. “The potion you hold does not grant joy or immortality to those who keep it. Its power lies in the act of giving. Share it wisely, for only then will its strength endure.”

The words settled like seeds in fertile ground. Indra and Agni carried the chalice back to the celestial realm, where they poured its essence into the rivers, letting it flow to every corner of existence. Life surged anew—gods regained their vigor, mortals found hope, and the vitality of the cosmos was restored.

In the quiet that followed, Indra stood beside Agni, gazing at the restored heavens. “We faced illusions, storms, and doubt,” he said. “But it was focus and determination that brought us here.”

Agni nodded. "Purpose gave us clarity. Determination carried us forward. Without them, the potion would have been lost to us."

From that day, the energy of Vishakha was revered as a reminder that scattered effort leads to ruin, but focus transforms chaos into meaning. Determination, like Agni's flames, births success not through force, but through resilience. And so, Vishakha's message —"Focus transforms the scattered into the meaningful. Determination births success."—echoed through the cosmos, guiding all who sought purpose.

Moral of the Story

True success comes not from merely seeking power or glory but from acting with focus and purpose. Determination transforms obstacles into opportunities, and the greatest rewards are those shared for the greater good.

Modern-Day Relevance

In today's fast-paced world, distractions and challenges abound. The tale of Indra and Agni teaches us to stay focused on meaningful goals and to persevere with clarity of purpose.

> Professionally: Leaders can achieve lasting success by aligning their focus and efforts with the long term success of the organisation and of their teams, rather than pursuing personal ambition.

> Personally: Individuals facing overwhelming challenges can find strength in focusing on their

core values and remaining steadfast in their efforts.

Socially: Communities thrive when their members work together with determination and selflessness, transforming shared struggles into collective progress.

Vishakha's energy reminds us that focus and determination illuminate our path, even in the face of chaos and doubt, leading us toward meaningful and transformative success.

Real-Life Analogies for the New Seekers

1. Analogy: Preparing for the first 10K run

Imagine someone training for their first 10km run. Distractions abound—friends urging them to skip training, self-doubt whispering they'll never make it, and the temptation of comfort over effort. Yet, with focus on their goal and determination to finish, they push through physical and mental challenges. On race day, their perseverance pays off —not just in crossing the finish line, but in the sense of achievement and growth they gain from the journey.
Takeaway: Staying focused on meaningful goals and persevering through challenges transforms struggles into triumphs.

---

2. Analogy: Leading a Team Through a Crisis

Consider a team leader navigating a business challenge, such as declining sales or operational

hurdles. The leader resists the lure of quick fixes or personal gain, instead focusing on the team's collective mission. By staying determined and working collaboratively, the team identifies innovative solutions that not only resolve the immediate issue but strengthen their long-term strategy.
Takeaway: Leadership grounded in focus and selfless determination leads to solutions that benefit the collective, mirroring Indra and Agni's purpose-driven quest.

Practical Exercises for the Lunar Mansion

1. Visualization: The Archer's Focus

Close your eyes and imagine yourself as an archer standing in a serene forest. Before you is a target glowing with purpose, representing your highest goal. Feel the weight of the bow in your hands and the tension of the string as you draw it back with unwavering focus. Release the arrow, watching it fly straight and true toward the target, a symbol of your determination and success.

2. Journaling Prompt

Reflect on a goal or aspiration that is deeply important to you.

> What steps have you taken toward achieving it?
>
> What distractions or challenges are pulling you away, and how can you refocus?

Write about a time when determination helped you overcome a significant obstacle. What did you learn from that experience?

3. Action for the Day

Take one concrete step toward a goal you've been working on, no matter how small. Whether it's researching, making a call, or setting up a plan, let this action affirm your focus and determination.

Advanced Exercises to Harness the Energy of Vishakha

a) Meditation with Sound

Purpose: Align with Vishakha's energy of focus and determination.

Meditate for 15 minutes to bowstring sounds and the release of arrows. Imagine the arrows sharpening your focus and determination as they hit their mark.

b) Connect to Nature

Purpose: Embody Vishakha's energy of purpose and clarity.

Spend time observing a tree in bloom, noting how its branches extend toward the sun and sky while its roots hold firm. Reflect on how focus and determination help you grow toward your goals while staying grounded in your values.

c) Perform a Service

Purpose: Inspire determination in others.

Help someone clarify their own goals or support them in taking a step forward. This could mean sharing advice, encouraging their efforts, or simply listening to their aspirations and cheering them on. Do not expect anything in return.

"Focus gathers the scattered light of your being into a fire that forges destiny."

LUNAR MANSION 17: ANURADHA

In the shimmering depths of the Scorpius constellation, three stars—**Beta, Delta, and Pi Scorpii**—form a celestial bond that mirrors the essence of Anuradha. Known as the Lunar Mansion of **devotion** and **compassion**, it carries the **lotus** as its sacred symbol, a mark of purity rising above the murky waters of existence. Governed by **Saturn** and nestled within the embrace of the zodiac **Scorpio (ruler Mars)**, this nakshatra whispers of the unyielding strength found in connection and friendship. **"In compassion lies strength,"** it reminds us, **"and through connection, the soul's deepest needs are nurtured."**

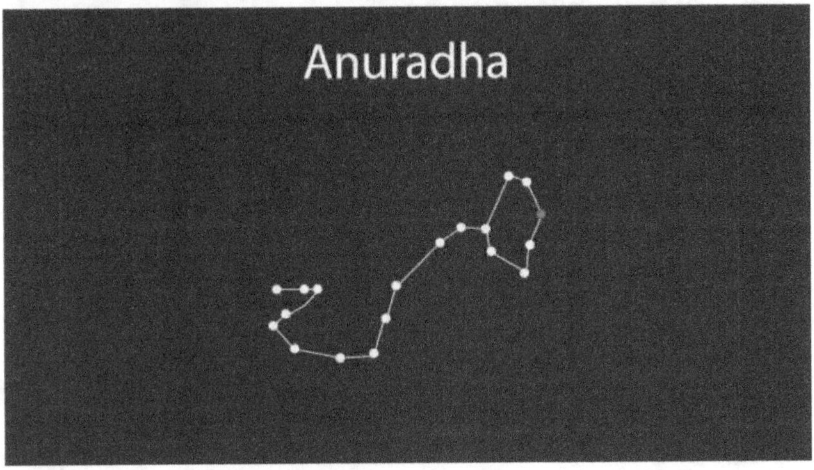

Image Source: https://popularvedicscience.com/astrology/anuradha-nakshatra

The Tale of Devotion and the Lotus of Compassion

The Context

Across the world, devotion is often misinterpreted as

blind faith or servitude. However, devotion is a profound and transformative force that fosters unity, resilience, and joy. The Nakshatra Anuradha is associated with this theme, emphasizing devotion and friendship as pathways to fulfilling the soul's deepest needs. Anuradha means the one *'causing well-being'* or *'the one following Radha.'*

The story of *Radha** and *Krishna**, central figures in Indian mythology, illustrates this beautifully. Radha's devotion transcends personal attachment, inspiring connection and harmony even in times of absence. Through her selflessness and resilience, Radha shows that true love and devotion are boundless, creating ripples of joy and harmony that uplift everyone.

The Story

The heavens glittered with stars, their light narrating stories of connection across the cosmos. Among them, none shone as vividly as Radha, a celestial being whose devotion to Krishna, the divine cowherd, was both her strength and her song. Her love wasn't confined to Krishna's presence; it flowed outward, nurturing harmony among the gods and celestial beings alike. Through her connection with him, Radha had become a quiet force that held the fabric of their celestial home together.

Yet harmony, like the stars themselves, is vulnerable to shadow. Whispers began to thread through the heavens, planted by Narada, the mischievous celestial sage. "Radha's devotion is beautiful," he mused to the gods, "but can it endure? What is love without its object? Can she thrive even in Krishna's absence?"

Curiosity sparked among the gods, and they devised a test. Through divine illusion, they hid Krishna from the celestial realm. His flute fell silent, and the joy that had once radiated through the heavens dimmed. The gods watched closely, expecting Radha to falter.

But Radha did not collapse into grief. She felt Krishna's absence acutely, as if a vital element of her being had been eliminated. Yet, rather than retreat into despair, she poured herself into the connections around her. She spoke to the stars, sang to the rivers, and tended to other beings who, too, seemed lost without Krishna's music.

Her sorrow found form in quiet acts of compassion. She wove garlands of jasmine for those who grieved and listened to the fears of the restless. Her love for Krishna, though tested, refused to shrink; instead, it expanded to touch everyone.

One evening, seated by a celestial river, Radha stared into its shimmering depths. The water reflected her longing, but also something deeper—a quiet resilience that glimmered just beneath. A tear escaped her eye, landing softly in the current. To her surprise, a golden lotus unfurled where the tear had fallen, its petals aglow. Another tear fell, and another lotus bloomed. Soon, the river brimmed with golden blossoms, their fragrance lifting the weight from the air.

Radha gathered the flowers in her arms, their warmth a reminder that Krishna's presence, though absent, still lived in her love. She carried them to the beings, who had grown silent and withdrawn. Offering each a golden lotus, she said, “These are not symbols of absence. They are reminders that love, when shared, can create beauty even in longing.”

The heavens began to brighten as the gods witnessed her quiet strength. The bonds Radha had nurtured began to repair the cracks left by Krishna’s absence. Laughter returned, carried by winds that once only sighed. The gods, humbled, saw what they had overlooked. “Even without Krishna’s presence,” they said, “Radha’s love inspires connection and strength. Her devotion is not tethered to need but grows through compassion.”

It was then that Krishna returned, his presence filling the heavens with music and light once more. In his arms, he carried the golden lotuses Radha had gifted to others. “You have shown me the highest form of devotion,” he said. “It is not in yearning or possession but in the love that strengthens and nurtures all.”

Radha smiled, her heart no longer heavy but luminous. Her journey had revealed what lay at the core of her love —not Krishna’s physical presence, but the strength it gave her to connect, to heal, and to inspire others.

As the gods celebrated their reunion, far below, a humble woman on Earth knelt in prayer, her heart weary from life’s burdens. Radha, sensing the sincerity of the woman’s longing, sent a golden lotus drifting down to her. When the woman found it, she felt her spirit renew, her strength rekindle. From that day, it was said that golden lotuses bloomed in the presence of unconditional love and the bonds forged through compassion.

In Radha's story, the heavens remembered a truth: "In compassion lies strength. Connection with others nurtures the soul's deepest needs." And so, the stars continued to sing, their light a testament to love's enduring power.

Moral of the Story

Love in the form of devotion is not about dependency or possession; it is about connection, selflessness, and inspiring others. True strength lies in loving deeply and sharing that love to nurture harmony, even in the face of separation or hardship.

Modern-Day Relevance

In today's world, where relationships often face challenges of time, distance, and misunderstandings, the lesson of Anuradha is profoundly relevant:

> Professionally: Devotion is about uplifting one another rather than clinging or expecting reciprocity. Whether in friendships or romantic relationships, focusing on selfless connection creates enduring harmony.
>
> Personally: When life feels like it has "taken Krishna away," focus on acts of kindness and connection to others. This helps sustain your spirit and rebuilds harmony, much like Radha's golden lotuses transformed the heavens.
>
> Spiritually: Devotion to a shared cause or group, like volunteering or supporting a friend in need, fosters resilience and joy not just within you but in

those you uplift.

Devotion isn't about dependence or proximity—it's about the energy we give to connect, inspire, and create harmony. Whether in personal relationships, friendships, or your community, devotion as selfless connection strengthens both you and those around you. Like Radha, you can inspire resilience and joy, even in moments of separation or uncertainty.

Real-Life Analogies for New Seekers

1. Real-Life Analogy: A Parent's Devotion to Their Child

A parent's love for their child often exemplifies selfless devotion. Imagine a parent guiding their child through life, celebrating their milestones, and offering support during tough times—even when the child is far away. The bond remains unbroken because the love is rooted in care and connection, not in physical proximity or personal gain.

Key Takeaway: Like Radha's devotion to Krishna, a parent's love is expansive and unconditional, creating a foundation of strength and harmony for the family.

---

2. Real-Life Analogy: A Friendship That Endures Distance

Think of two close friends separated by geography. Despite not meeting often, they maintain their bond through heartfelt conversations, acts of kindness, and mutual encouragement. Their friendship thrives because it's built on trust and selflessness, not on constant interaction.

Key Takeaway: Radha's golden lotuses symbolize the beauty and resilience of such friendships. Even in separation, the connection inspires growth and joy for both individuals and those around them.

Practical Exercises for the Lunar Mansion

1. Visualization: The Circle of Devotion

Close your eyes and imagine yourself standing in a glowing circle of light surrounded by people who uplift and support you. Feel the warmth of their love and the strength of your connection. Visualize yourself offering them the same devotion and kindness, creating a harmonious and nurturing bond that grows stronger with each passing moment.

2. Journaling Prompt

Reflect on the relationships in your life that bring you the deepest sense of connection and devotion.

> What makes these relationships meaningful?
>
> How can you strengthen these bonds further?

Write about a time when your devotion to a person, cause, or goal brought you fulfillment. What did it teach you about the power of connection?

3. Action for the Day

Perform an act of devotion today. This could be spending quality time with a loved one, supporting a friend in need, or offering kindness to someone without expecting anything in return. Let this action deepen your connections.

Advanced Exercises to Harness the Energy of Anuradha

a) Meditation with Sound

Purpose: Align with Anuradha's energy of devotion and friendship.

Meditate for 15 minutes to harmonious chanting with tambourine jingles. Visualize these sounds deepening your devotion and strengthening your connections.

b) Connect to Nature

Purpose: Embrace Anuradha's nurturing and loyal essence.

Spend time observing a flock of birds or animals that move together in harmony, reflecting the power of connection and mutual support. Reflect on how your connections help you grow and thrive.

c) Perform a Service

Purpose: Foster devotion and friendship in someone's life.

Help a friend or loved one with a task or offer emotional support to someone facing challenges. Do not expect anything in return. Your act of devotion will strengthen your bond and align you with Anuradha's energy.

"Devotion is the bridge between souls; its strength lies in the giving, not the receiving."

LUNAR MANSION 18: JYESHTHA

In the heart of the celestial **scorpion**, Jyeshtha **(Alpha Scorpii, or Antares)** burns as a fiery testament to the burdens and brilliance of seniority and leadership. Marked by its symbol—**a circular amulet or umbrella**—and governed by **Mercury**, Jyeshtha sits in the relentless zodiac of **Scorpio**, ruled by **Mars**. Here, the cosmos speaks of an elder's journey: wisdom tempered by trials, and responsibility wielded with the grace of humility. **True power**, it reminds us, **does not roar—it serves, quietly etching its legacy in the lives it touches.** The spiritual theme of Jyeshtha calls us to **rise above pride, embracing the delicate balance of guidance and servitude.**

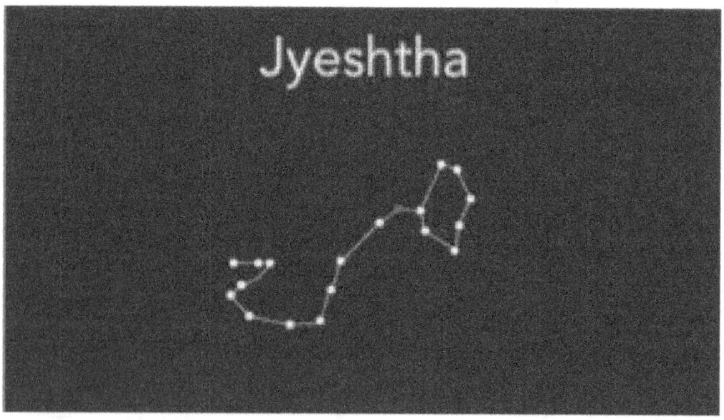

Image Source: https://popularvedicscience.com/astrology/jyeshta-nakshatra

---

The Tale of Indra and the Crown of Wisdom

Context for Readers

In Indian mythology, Indra is the king of the gods, ruling

the celestial realm with power and justice. This story, intertwined with themes of wisdom and responsibility, reflects the timeless struggles of leadership—balancing authority with humility. The 18th lunar mansion, Jyeshtha, embodies these lessons, emphasizing that true power lies not in dominance but in selfless service. This tale of Indra and his journey to rediscover wisdom resonates universally, offering guidance for leaders across cultures and contexts.

The Story

High in the heavens, Indra sat on his golden throne, his Crown of *Svarga* (heaven) resting upon his brow. The celestial jewels embedded in it glimmered faintly, their light subdued, as though mirroring the unease that clung to the air. Around him, the court bustled with the familiar rhythms of divine life—*devas** (celestial beings) offering praises, musicians weaving celestial melodies, and sages speaking of distant prophecies. Yet, the weight of the crown pressed heavier than usual.

Indra's gaze wandered to the Mirror of Svarga, an artifact that reflected not just the appearance but the essence of its beholder. He stared into it and saw not the confident ruler he once knew, but a figure cloaked in doubt. His shoulders sagged under the invisible concern. "I am the king of the gods," he thought. "Why does my own reflection feel like a stranger?"

Whispers stirred in the court like a quiet breeze. "The crown dims," some murmured. "The light of its wisdom fades." Though spoken softly, the words reached Indra's ears, each one a thorn in his pride.

Narada, the celestial sage, entered the court that day, his expression a mixture of mischief and insight. "O Indra," Narada began, "your court brims with splendor, yet your heart seems heavy. Why do you bear this burden?"

Indra bristled. "I carry the weight of leadership. I rule with strength and justice!"

Narada's eyes twinkled with knowing amusement. "Strength and justice are mighty, but a crown does not shine by power alone. It gleams when wisdom tempers its authority. Perhaps you have forgotten why you wear it."

Indra's voice sharpened. "Forgotten? I am the guardian of balance, the wielder of the Vajra (a thunderbolt weapon). What more is required of me?"

Narada gestured toward the horizon. "O King, if you seek clarity, journey to the Pond of Reflection. There, answers will find you."

Reluctantly, Indra descended from his opulent court into the ethereal Pond of Reflection. The air here was infused with the scent of earth and ancient truths. Shadows moved with an intention of their own, and each step carried him deeper into its embrace.

In a nearby clearing shrouded in mist, Indra encountered a serpent coiled around a gnarled tree. Its eyes glowed with quiet menace as it hissed, "What is strength without utility?"

Indra gripped his Vajra and struck, but the serpent dissolved into the mist, leaving its question lingering in the air.

Further ahead, a bird of radiant plumage perched atop a smooth stone. Its voice was as clear as a mountain spring as it sang, "What is power without humility?"

Indra reached for the bird, but it exploded into a burst of light, its melody trailing after him like an unanswered riddle.

Frustration brewed within him, a tempest of pride and confusion. He pressed on, arriving at the destination. There, by the still Pond of Reflection, sat an old, blind man, his presence unassuming yet magnetic. Indra felt an inexplicable pull toward him.

"What wisdom do you seek, king of the gods?" the man asked, his voice steady and timeless.

Indra hesitated before speaking. "I wear the Crown of Svarga, yet its weight grows heavier. I do not understand why."

The old man gestured toward the pond. "Look into the water, not at your reflection but beyond it."

Indra knelt and gazed into the pond. At first, he saw his regal form, adorned with the trappings of power. But as the ripples settled, the image shifted. He saw the devas (gods) in his court, their eyes filled with expectation. He saw the Earth, parched and waiting for rain. He saw mortals, praying for guidance and sustenance. And then he saw himself—not the protector he believed himself to be, but a figure ensnared by pride, distant and unyielding.

The realization struck like the thunderbolt he wielded. "My crown does not make me a king. My actions do.

Leadership is not dominance but duty, and power is a gift to serve, not a right to wield."

The old man spoke again, his tone soft yet firm. "Wisdom is not found in strength, Indra. True power lies in humility, in leading not for yourself but for those you serve."

Indra bowed his head, his voice trembling. "You have shown me the way. Thank you."

When he rose, the old man was gone, and the pond shimmered with golden light. In his place lay the Crown of Svarga, now radiating a brilliance it had not held in centuries. Indra lifted it and placed it upon his head. It felt lighter, not because its weight had changed, but because his heart had.

Returning to Svarga, Indra entered his court, but this time his presence was different. He listened with patience, spoke with humility, and acted not to assert his power but to uplift those who depended on him. His court murmured in awe. "The crown shines once more," they said.

From that day forward, the devas no longer feared their king's pride. They trusted his wisdom, for it was born not of power but of purpose. And the Crown of Svarga gleamed, its light a testament to a ruler who had learned that true power serves others, and true wisdom leads with humility.

Moral of the Story

A high position or true leadership are not about

dominance but about service. Wisdom is not in holding power but in wielding it with humility, compassion, and responsibility. A leader shines brightest when they put the needs of others above their pride.

Modern-Day Relevance

In today's world, leadership is often equated with authority and control. Indra's story reminds us that:

> Professionally: A leader who leads by example and prioritizes their team's growth becomes a respected leader. By valuing input and supporting their team, they inspire loyalty and collective success.
>
> Personally: In relationships, controlling behavior can lead to resentment. Mutual respect and shared decision-making create stronger, healthier connections.
>
> Socially: Influential figures who use their platforms to uplift marginalized communities exemplify the essence of Jyeshtha. Their actions remind us that true legacy is built through service and compassion.

Jyeshtha's energy teaches that wisdom tempers pride, and leadership shines brightest when it is driven by service. Whether in professional or personal spheres, humility transforms power into a force for growth, harmony, and inspiration.

Real-Life Analogies for the New Seekers

1. The Corporate Leader Who Listens

Imagine a corporate CEO who initially believes their success stems solely from their decisions and authority. Over time, they face challenges —employee dissatisfaction, declining productivity, and resistance to change. Through self-reflection and feedback, they realize that true leadership requires empathy and service. By listening to their team, empowering individuals, and fostering collaboration, they transform their company's culture and results.

Takeaway: Leadership is most impactful when it is grounded in humility and a genuine desire to uplift others.

---

2. A Parent's Journey

A parent initially believes their role is to direct and control their child's life. Over time, they see that their child thrives not under control but through encouragement and guidance. By stepping back and supporting their child's unique strengths, the parent fosters confidence and growth in their child while strengthening their bond.

Takeaway: True power in relationships comes from understanding and serving others, not asserting dominance.

Practical Exercises for the Lunar Mansion

1. Visualization: The Crown of Wisdom

Close your eyes and picture yourself ascending

a majestic mountain. At the peak, you find a glowing crown placed on a pedestal, symbolizing the wisdom and responsibility you have earned through life's trials. Visualize yourself wearing the crown, feeling its weight as a reminder of your power to lead with humility and wisdom.

2. Journaling Prompt

Reflect on a time when you were in a position of leadership or responsibility.

> How did you approach this role?
>
> What lessons did you learn about humility and service?

Write about an area of your life where you feel called to take on greater responsibility. What steps can you take to lead with wisdom and integrity?

3. Action for the Day

Step into a leadership role today, even in a small way. Whether it's guiding a group project, helping a group of colleagues, or organizing a family activity, focus on serving others with humility and wisdom.

Advanced Exercises to Harness the Energy of Jyeshtha

a) Meditation with Sound

> Purpose: Connect with Jyeshtha's energy of wisdom and leadership.
>
> Meditate for 15 minutes to low, thunderous drumbeats with pauses. Let the beats evoke

wisdom and humility, helping you lead with integrity.

b) Connect to Nature

Purpose: Embody Jyeshtha's sense of resilience and responsibility.

Spend time near a tall, ancient tree or a high vantage point, such as a hill or mountain. Reflect on its strength and endurance, and how it offers stability to everything around it. Let this inspire your own leadership qualities.

c) Perform a Service

Purpose: Use Jyeshtha's energy to uplift others.

Mentor someone or offer guidance to someone in need of direction. Share your knowledge or wisdom to help them overcome a challenge or achieve a goal. Do not expect anything in return.

"Wisdom is the crown of humility; power finds its highest purpose in service to others."

LUNAR MANSION 19: MOOLA

Beneath the infinite canopy of the night, where the stars of **Lambda, Mu, Zeta, Eta, Theta, and Iota Sagittarii** illuminate the heavens, lies the secret of Moola—**'tied bundle of roots.'** This Nakshatra, governed by **Ketu (South Node)**, anchors us to life's unspoken truths while urging us to unravel its deepest mysteries. Rooted in the zodiac of **Sagittarius**, the domain of **Jupiter**, Moola represents the eternal quest for clarity in a universe of paradoxes.

In the sacred embrace of this Lunar Mansion, we are reminded: **"Truth lies at the roots. To rise high, dig deep into what grounds you."** Moola does not merely invite exploration; it demands that we confront the unseen forces shaping our lives and unearth the foundation that sustains our journey.

Note for Astronomy enthusiasts: When viewing from the earth, the center of our galaxy, the Milky Way, is in the same line as Moola nakshatra. This galactic center is an intense area of radiation and activity, housing a massive black hole. Hence the name Moola (meaning *root* or *source*), which indicates that it is the source of all energy for our galaxy. It is a point of destruction of the old and rebirth of new elements of our galaxy. Spiritually, this cosmic gateway radiates powerful energies that influence higher consciousness and spiritual awakening.

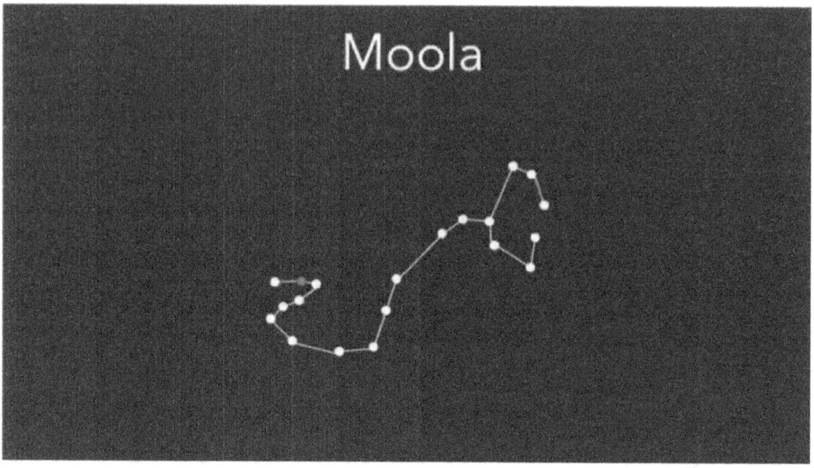

Image Source: https://popularvedicscience.com/astrology/mula-nakshatra

The Tale of Satyavan and the Roots of Truth

Context for Readers

Indian mythology often intertwines celestial wisdom with human experiences, creating stories that guide seekers on life's deeper truths. The Nakshatras, or lunar mansions, are 27 constellations that represent different aspects of life's journey. Moola, the 19th Nakshatra, is associated with rootedness and the quest for truth —a reminder that life's greatest strengths arise from grounding ourselves in what truly matters.

This myth-inspired tale of Satyavan and Savitri, an important tale in Indian mythology, exemplifies this theme. It highlights resilience, love, and the pursuit of truth in the face of life's inevitable cycles. Through this story, readers are invited to explore the deeper roots of existence, where real clarity and strength are found.

The Story

In a forest so ancient that its very roots seemed to cradle the stories of time, Satyavan lived in quiet exile with his parents. Once a prince, his family had been cast out of their kingdom by treachery, and they now called the wilderness their home. But Satyavan found solace among the towering trees and whispering winds. His days were spent in the rhythm of nature—gathering fruits and roots, tending to the land, and embracing the simple life the forest offered.

One morning, as he dug into the soft earth for roots, a flicker of light caught his attention. Turning, he saw a young woman stepping lightly among the trees, her presence both regal and serene. Savitri, a princess drawn by an inexplicable pull, had ventured deep into the woods. Their eyes met, and the world around them seemed to pause.

"Who are you?" she asked, her voice lilting like the wind through leaves. "And why do you labor this way?"

"I am Satyavan," he replied, his hands stained with soil. "Once, I lived in a palace. Now, I live among the roots."

Savitri smiled, her gaze unwavering. "Roots sustain life. They are far more precious than jewels."

A bond grew swiftly between them, as unshakable as the ancient trees. Against the wishes of her family, Savitri chose to marry Satyavan, leaving behind the grandeur of her palace for the quiet strength of the forest. Yet, their happiness was shadowed by a prophecy: a sage foretold that Satyavan would die within a year.

Savitri did not flinch. "If death comes, I will walk beside him to meet it."

The days passed like fleeting whispers, each moment shared with quiet purpose. On the fateful day, beneath the sprawling shade of a banyan tree, Satyavan's breath faltered. He collapsed, life draining from him like water slipping through cupped hands. Savitri cradled him, her heart trembling but her resolve as steadfast as the earth beneath her feet.

As the sun dipped low, the air grew heavy, and from the shadows emerged *Yama*[*], the god of death. Draped in robes darker than the night, he approached with a presence that was both solemn and unyielding.

"Savitri," Yama said, his voice deep as the roots of the earth. "Your husband's time has come."

Savitri rose, meeting his gaze without fear. "If his path ends here, then I will walk it with him."

Yama paused, intrigued by her devotion. "Few would dare follow me into the shadowed realms. Do you realise what you are asking for?"

"I know that the roots of life and death are intertwined. To leave him now would be to lose my own grounding."

Yama permitted her to follow, and together they journeyed through valleys of silence and clouds of flickering shadows. With every step, Savitri's feet ached, but her spirit held firm.

Finally, they came to the World Tree, its roots stretching

endlessly into the cosmos. "If you seek to change what cannot be changed," Yama said, "dig here. Discover what lies at the roots."

Kneeling before the immense tree, Savitri plunged her hands into the earth. The soil was cool and damp, clinging to her fingers as she dug deeper and deeper. She unearthed no treasure, no secrets hidden in gold or jewels. Instead, she saw her reflection in the roots—her love, her sacrifices, her strength, and her fears. She saw the cycles of life and death, not as adversaries, but as companions in an eternal dance. Misfortune, she realized, was not something to be fought against but something to face with steady resolve.

Yama's voice broke the stillness. "You have unearthed the truth, Savitri. Life rises because it is rooted in the soil of loss. You do not hold on by resisting the cycle, but by honoring its balance."

He extended his hands, Satyavan's soul glimmering within them. "Take him. He is yours once more."

As Yama faded into the shadows, Satyavan stirred in her arms. His eyes opened, and he smiled weakly, as though waking from a long, dark dream. Together, they returned to the banyan tree, its roots strong and its branches reaching toward the heavens.

In the years that followed, the banyan tree became sacred ground, a place where those lost in life's storms could come to find their grounding. As events unfolded, Satyavan and Savitri rebuilt their kingdom, their reign marked not by conquest but by compassion, their legacy as deep and enduring as the roots that had shown them the truth.

For those who sought the banyan tree's shade, its presence whispered a simple yet profound truth: "To rise high, dig deep into what grounds you."

Moral of the Story

True strength lies in grounding ourselves in the truth, no matter how painful or challenging the journey. By seeking the roots of existence, we find the clarity and resilience to rise above any trial.

Modern-Day Relevance

In today's fast-paced world, people often look for quick solutions, skimming the surface of their challenges without addressing the roots:

> Professionally: In career setbacks, people often focus on external factors—blaming market trends or team inefficiencies. Moola's wisdom reminds us to dig deeper, examining personal habits, skills, or decision-making to identify what truly needs adjustment.
>
> Personally: Relationships often falter because people address surface issues like arguments or time spent together without exploring deeper roots like trust, communication, or shared values. By addressing these foundational aspects, relationships can grow stronger and more fulfilling.
>
> Spiritually: In a world filled with distractions, grounding practices like meditation, mindfulness,

or spending time in nature help reconnect us with our core. This rootedness provides clarity and resilience in the face of life's uncertainties.

Moola's story and insight teach us that true strength lies in addressing the core of our challenges, not just their symptoms. By grounding ourselves in the roots of truth, we can rise above life's trials with clarity, balance, and purpose. Like Savitri, digging deep not only saves us from despair but also strengthens our ability to thrive.

Real-Life Analogies for the New Seekers

1. The Foundation of a Treehouse:

Imagine building a treehouse. The higher you want it to soar, the stronger and deeper the tree's roots must grow. If you neglect the foundation and focus only on the visible structure, it will collapse under pressure.

Key Lesson: Like Savitri digging deep into the roots of truth, we must strengthen our foundations—whether in personal values, relationships, or skills—before reaching for greater heights.

2. Resolving Workplace Challenges:

A team at work struggles to meet deadlines because of constant miscommunication. Instead of addressing superficial symptoms like speed or tools, the leader dives deep into the root issue: lack of clarity in roles and expectations. By solving the foundational problem, the team begins to thrive.

Key Lesson: Tackling root causes, rather than quick

fixes, leads to sustainable solutions and progress.

Practical Exercises for the Lunar Mansion

1. Visualization: The Roots of Truth

Close your eyes and imagine yourself as a mighty banyan or oak with deep, expansive roots anchoring you to the Earth. Visualize these roots digging deeper into the soil, uncovering buried treasures of truth and wisdom. As you connect with the deepest layers, feel yourself becoming grounded, steady, and enlightened by the hidden truths you uncover.

2. Journaling Prompt

Reflect on an area of your life where you seek deeper understanding or clarity.

> What questions have been lingering in your mind?
>
> What steps can you take to uncover the truth?

Write about a time when facing a hard truth brought you personal growth. How did it change your perspective or strengthen your resolve?

3. Action for the Day

Commit to digging deeper into an area of your life today. This could mean having an honest conversation, researching a topic you've avoided, or spending time reflecting on a difficult situation. Let this action guide you toward clarity and growth.

Advanced Exercises to Harness the Energy of Moola

a) Meditation with Sound

Purpose: Align with Moola's energy of rootedness and seeking truth.

Meditate for 15 minutes to the resonant hum of a didgeridoo. Picture the deep vibrations rooting you firmly while revealing hidden truths.

b) Connect to Nature

Purpose: Embody essence of grounding , seeking.

Spend time near the roots of a tree or a plant. Observe how the roots hold the tree steady while seeking nourishment from the Earth. Reflect on how you can similarly ground yourself while seeking deeper truths.

c) Perform a Service

Purpose: Share Moola's energy of uncovering truths with others.

Help someone resolve a deep-seated issue or support them in finding clarity. Whether it's through advice, research, or simply listening, assist them in uncovering their path forward. Do not expect anything in return.

"Truth lies buried in the roots of your being; dig deep, and you will find the foundation on which you stand."

LUNAR MANSION 20:PURVA ASHADHA

Within the radiant arch of Sagittarius, where stars like **Delta Sagittarii (Kaus Media), Epsilon Sagittarii (Kaus Australis), and Zeta Sagittarii (Kaus Borealis)** spell their magic, lies the energy of Purva Ashadha—a heavenly **winnowing basket or fan** (its symbol), ignited by **Venus** (nakshatra lord) and guided by the zodiac ruler **Jupiter's** wisdom. This is not just a starry formation in the heavens but a sanctuary of **invigoration** and **optimism**. Here, seeds of possibility rest, waiting to unfurl in the light of belief, their growth nurtured by the unwavering vitality of faith.

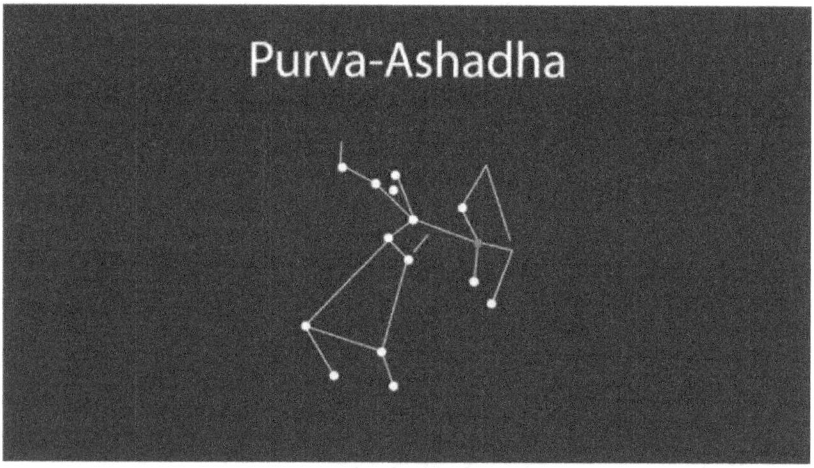

Image Source: https://popularvedicscience.com/ astrology/purva-ashadha-nakshatra

---

The Warrior Queen and the Seeds of Invigoration

Context for Readers

In Vedic Astrology, the Nakshatra Purva Ashadha is

associated with invigoration, optimism, and triumph, symbolizing the power of belief and the potential for growth even in challenging times. Ruled by the goddess Apah, who governs water and renewal, this Nakshatra reflects the transformative power of hope and perseverance. The story of Queen Varini captures this essence, illustrating how faith and action can overcome despair and lead to flourishing.

The Story

Long ago, nestled along the vast Saraswati River, the kingdom of Shaktipur thrived under the rule of Queen Varini, a woman known for her wisdom and unyielding devotion to her people. The river's waters brought life to the land, turning fields lush and bountiful. But as with all blessings, the river's abundance was not infinite. One fateful year, the rains faltered. The Saraswati shrank, the fields cracked. Hunger and despair gripped the once-prosperous kingdom.

Faced with the specter of famine, Queen Varini sought counsel from the kingdom's sages. Their response was cryptic yet charged with purpose: "The goddess Apah, keeper of waters, dwells in the Sacred Grove of Invigoration. To seek her aid, you must journey through the Valley of Despair, where doubt festers, and hope falters. Only belief will light your way."

The queen's resolve was unshaken. "For my people, I will traverse even the deepest shadows," she declared. The chief sage handed her a small pouch of seeds. "Plant these where your heart feels hope," he instructed. "They will guide you."

Varini's journey began under a blazing sun, her steps echoing in the silence of the barren land. The once-green fields of her kingdom gave way to the Valley of Despair, a desolate expanse where the air felt heavy and shadows curled like grasping fingers.

As she ventured deeper, the valley seemed to speak, its whispers slithering into her mind. "What if you fail? What if your kingdom is beyond saving?" The doubts tightened around her like vines, each step harder than the last. The seeds in her hand felt small, insignificant.

Then, a memory surfaced: a farmer from her kingdom, his hands calloused yet gentle as he tilled the soil, saying, "It begins with a seed, Your Majesty. Even the smallest seed holds the promise of a harvest."

Clutching the first seed, Varini knelt and pressed it into the cracked earth. "Hope is my light," she murmured.

To her astonishment, a delicate sprout emerged instantly, its leaves shimmering faintly in the dim air. The sprout pointed ahead, as if urging her onward. Encouraged, she took another step.

Each time the valley's shadows grew darker, Varini planted another seed. Doubt pressed closer, its whispers more insistent. "What if the sprouts wither? What if this is all in vain?" But each time, she recalled her people's trust in her, their faces lined with hunger yet shining with faith.

Each seed brought a new sprout, their glow forming a luminous path through the valley's desolation. As the trail grew, so did Varini's conviction. The valley's whispers faded, overpowered by the quiet strength of her belief.

At last, she emerged from the valley, where the air turned sweet and alive. Before her lay the Sacred Grove, a sanctuary of vibrant greens and flowing streams. In its heart stood Apah, the goddess of waters, her presence serene yet commanding.

"You have come far, Queen Varini," Apah said, her voice like the first raindrop in a drought. "But know this: invigoration is not found at the journey's end. It grows in the seeds of belief you plant along the way."

Apah extended a chalice filled with water that shimmered with life itself. "Drink, and the waters shall return to your kingdom. But beware—the storms of doubt are not easily quelled."

As Varini raised the chalice, the ground trembled. Dark clouds swirled above, and a voice roared, "Hope is fragile! It cannot endure the weight of despair!" Her hands shook, and the chalice slipped, its water spilling into the dry soil.

Varini froze, her heart heavy with the weight of failure. But then she saw it: the ground where the water had fallen began to stir. A single sprout pushed through the soil, its green vibrant against the gray earth. She knelt, her fingers brushing the tender leaves, and whispered, "Hope is not fragile. It is the seed of all that thrives."

Scooping the remaining water with her hands, she poured it onto the sprout. The grove erupted in life. Flowers bloomed in radiant colors, streams gushed from the earth, and the air filled with the hum of renewal.

Apah smiled, her eyes bright with approval.

"You have shown that belief is the source of all growth," the goddess said, handing Varini a vessel of eternal water. "Take this, and let your kingdom flourish once more."

When Varini returned, the kingdom rejoiced as the Saraswati River roared back to life. The land healed, and the people celebrated their queen's courage and faith. Yet the greatest marvel lay not in the river's renewal but in the seeds Varini had planted in the valley. They had grown into golden plants, their leaves etched with shimmering inscriptions:

"In doubt, find faith. In despair, sow hope."

These plants became sacred symbols, reminders of the queen's journey and the truth she had uncovered: that belief, no matter how small, holds the power to transform barren soil into a garden of possibilities.

Generations passed, but the golden plants endured, their wisdom inspiring all who saw them. The kingdom of Shaktipur flourished not just because of the waters but because its people, like their queen, had learned to plant their seeds in the light of belief.

Moral of the Story

Hope is the seed of transformation, and belief is the water that nurtures it. By planting optimism even in barren times, we create the foundation for renewal and growth.

Modern-Day Relevance

In the fast-paced and often uncertain world we live in,

people frequently face moments of doubt and despair —whether it's dealing with career setbacks, personal challenges, or global crises. Queen Varini's story reminds us that:

Professionally: When a career setback occurs, such as missing a promotion or facing a failed project, optimism and adaptability can turn the experience into a foundation for greater achievements.

Personally: During times of personal loss or uncertainty, focusing on small steps forward—like reaching out to loved ones or setting new goals—can lead to renewal and healing.

Socially: Addressing global challenges such as climate change requires collective optimism and action. Like Queen Varini's journey, belief in a better future and collective effort can create meaningful change.

Purva Ashadha's lesson for the modern seeker is clear: optimism is not naive—it is transformative. By planting seeds of hope and watering them with belief, we can invigorate our lives and transform challenges into opportunities for growth.

Real-Life Analogies for the New Seekers

Analogy 1: A Gardener Reviving a Wilted Garden

Imagine a gardener whose beloved garden has withered during a long drought. Despair creeps in, but instead of giving up, they plant new seeds, watering them with the little water they have left.

Slowly, the seeds sprout, transforming the barren garden into a lush oasis.

Key Lesson: Just as the gardener believes in the potential of the seeds despite the drought, we must plant hope and nurture it with optimism, even in difficult times.

Analogy 2: An Entrepreneur Facing Setbacks

Picture an entrepreneur launching a new business that initially fails to gain traction. They face moments of doubt but decide to pivot and try again, fueled by a belief in their vision. Each small step—building new strategies, engaging with customers, and learning from mistakes—creates momentum. Eventually, the business thrives, becoming an example of resilience and innovation.

Key Lesson: Like the seeds in Varini's story, belief and action during challenging times can pave the way for success.

Practical Exercises for the Lunar Mansion

1. Visualization: The Rising Wave

Close your eyes and imagine yourself standing on a beach as a powerful yet gentle wave approaches. The wave represents your inner optimism and invigoration, carrying seeds of potential. As it washes over you, feel its energy filling you with enthusiasm and confidence. Visualize these seeds growing into opportunities and success.

2. Journaling Prompt

Reflect on an area of your life where you feel energized and optimistic.

What fuels this feeling?

How can you channel this energy into new opportunities?

Write about a time when your belief in yourself or a situation led to positive outcomes. How can you recreate that mindset now?

3. Action for the Day

Take a bold step today toward something you believe in. This could be starting a new project, sharing an idea, or reaching out to someone for collaboration. Let your optimism inspire action.

Advanced Exercises to Harness the Energy of Purva Ashadha

a) Meditation with Sound

Purpose: Align with Purva Ashadha's invigorating and optimistic energy.

Meditate for 15 minutes to bubbling water streams with light splashes. Imagine the bubbling energy invigorating you and nurturing optimism.

b) Connect to Nature

Purpose: Embody Purva Ashadha's refreshing and forward-moving essence.

Spend time near a body of moving water such as a river or ocean. Reflect on how water is always moving forward, adapting yet unstoppable. Let it inspire your own sense of invigoration and optimism.

c) Perform a Service

Purpose: Spread optimism and encouragement to others.

Support someone's endeavor or uplift them with your words. Offer your belief in their abilities or help them see possibilities they might have overlooked. Your optimism can ignite theirs. Do not expect anything in return.

"Optimism is the light that nurtures growth; even the weakest seed can thrive in its warmth."

LUNAR MANSION 21: UTTARA ASHADHA

Under the watchful gaze of the celestial guardians (stars)—**Phi, Zeta, Tau, and Sigma Sagittarii**—lies this mansion. Like the silent strength of the **Elephant's Tusk**, Uttara Ashadha draws its power from the blazing light of its planetary lord, **the Sun**, carving a path through the intertwined realms of **Sagittarius and Capricorn** (ruled by **Jupiter and Saturn**, respectively). This mansion whispers a timeless truth: **"Victory is earned through persistent effort and unwavering integrity."** It beckons the traveler to not merely dream but to endure, transforming trials into triumphs with each unyielding step.

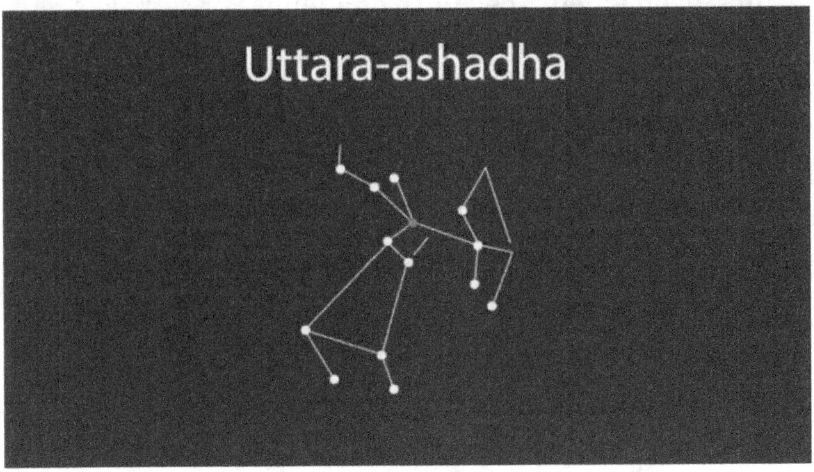

Image Source: https://popularvedicscience.com/astrology/uttara-ashadha-nakshatra

The Tale of Mahabali and the eternal Gift

Context for Readers

Indian mythology is rich with stories that blend cosmic principles and moral lessons, offering universal truths through allegories. This myth-inspired tale of Mahabali and Vamana originates from these traditions, highlighting the delicate balance between ambition and humility. Mahabali, a noble demon king, exemplifies leadership, generosity, and integrity, yet his unchecked ambition leads to a divine intervention by Vishnu, one of the principal deities tasked with maintaining cosmic order.

This story introduces Uttara Ashadha, the 21st lunar mansion, whose energy symbolizes victory through persistence and unwavering integrity. It reminds readers that true triumphs are not always immediate or grandiose—they emerge from staying steadfast in one's values, even when faced with challenges or setbacks.

The Story

The heavens tremored with unease, their tranquility disturbed by the steady rise of Mahabali, the great *asura**(demon) king. His reign on Earth was unlike any other before. His kingdom flourished with abundance. No stomach went hungry, no talent lay dormant. His relentless dedication built bridges between prosperity and justice, crafting a utopia where every citizen thrived.

Yet, his brilliance cast long shadows. In the celestial realms, the gods grew restless, their murmurs of disquiet spread by the winds. Indra, king of the gods, clenched his golden scepter, his gaze stormy. "Mahabali's power rises in an unchecked manner. Soon, his light will outshine ours. What if he aspires to rule over the heavens as well?" The gods turned to Vishnu, the preserver of the universe, for guidance.

Vishnu, ever composed, spoke with calm certainty. "Mahabali is not wicked, but even noble ambition must bow to balance. He must learn that true victory is not in dominion but in humility and the strength to persist with integrity."

In the earthly palace of Mahabali, preparations for a grand *yajna** (fire ritual) were underway. The scent of sandalwood and camphor wove through the air as priests chanted sacred verses. The ritual was a testament to Mahabali's dedication to his people, a celebration of the kingdom's prosperity. As the flames of the sacred fire crackled, a figure stepped into the gathering—a young dwarf sage, his presence understated but magnetic. His name was Vamana.

The court quieted. Mahabali, his demeanor ever gracious, stepped forward. "Welcome, holy one. How may I serve you?"

Vamana's voice was calm, his gaze steady. "I seek only the boon of land—enough to cover three steps."

The court erupted in laughter. How much could such a diminutive figure possibly claim? But Mahabali, bound by his integrity, silenced the murmurs with a raised hand.

"If three steps of land are what you desire, it shall be yours."

The moment his vow was spoken, the air in the hall shifted. Vamana began to grow in size, his form expanding into the cosmic beyond. His head pierced the heavens, his feet spanned the horizon, and his presence filled the skies.

With his first step, Vamana claimed the entirety of the Earth. With his second, he stretched across the heavens, leaving no realm untouched. He turned to Mahabali, his eyes steady, his voice resonating. "There is no land left for my third step. Where shall I place it? Or will you fail to honor your promise, O king ?"

Mahabali stood motionless, the despair of realization settling over him. This was no ordinary sage; this was Vishnu incarnate, who had come to test him. The king's face bore no trace of defiance, only a calm resolve. He knelt, bowing low. "Place your foot upon my head. I surrender to you and offer all that I have."

Vamana's colossal form paused, the gathered court holding its breath. With deliberate grace, the cosmic being placed his foot upon Mahabali's head, sending him to the underworld. The hall fell silent, but within Mahabali, a fire still burned. He rose in the dim realm, his shoulders upright.

"I have lost my throne and my lands," he declared, his voice resolute. "But my integrity and persistence still endure. That is my true victory."

Vamana, now returned to his dwarf-sage form and

observed the king's unwavering spirit. Touched by his resolve, Vishnu spoke through the dwarf-sage, his voice gentle but firm. "Mahabali, your humility and dedication shine brighter than any crown. As a boon, I grant you this: though you dwell in the underworld, you shall visit your people once every year till the end of time. They will honor you not as a ruler, but as a symbol of virtue and enduring effort."

From that day forward, the festival of Onam (mainly celebrated in Kerala, India) came to life, a celebration of Mahabali's spirit. Each year, as lamps flicker and joy fills the streets, the people welcome their king with open hearts, a living tribute to the lesson he embodied: Victory is earned not through conquest but through persistent effort and unwavering integrity.

In the quiet of the heavens, Vishnu watched as Mahabali's legacy endured, a reminder that the greatest triumphs are those that withstand even the humbling weight of surrender.

Moral of the Story

True victory is not measured by power or dominance but by the strength of one's character, the persistence to uphold values, and the humility to accept change. Mahabali's story shows us that even in apparent defeat, one can achieve greatness by staying true to one's integrity.

Modern-Day Relevance

In the modern world, Mahabali's journey resonates deeply:

Professionally: Leaders who stay committed to their ethical standards often inspire loyalty and respect. For example, a manager who prioritizes team well-being over short-term profits may not rise as quickly in the corporate ladder but creates a lasting impact and a legacy of trust.

Personally: Facing personal setbacks—like a breakup or losing a job—can feel like defeat. However, by accepting the situation gracefully and continuing to act with integrity, individuals often find opportunities for deeper self-awareness and new beginnings.

Socially: In a world where power dynamics often prioritize dominance, Mahabali's story highlights the importance of humility and selflessness. Communities thrive when collaboration and shared values take precedence over individual ambition.

Uttara Ashadha's energy teaches us that the greatest victories come not from overpowering others but from persisting in our principles, even when the odds seem insurmountable. Mahabali's story reminds us that integrity and humility light the path to true triumph.

Real-Life Analogies for the New Seekers

1. A Small Business Owner Facing Adversity
   Imagine a small business owner who starts with limited resources but persists through economic downturns, competition, and countless challenges. Despite setbacks, they uphold their principles—

treating employees fairly, providing quality service, and building trust. Even if they don't become the wealthiest in their industry, their legacy of integrity inspires respect and loyalty, ensuring long-term success.

Key Takeaway: True victory lies in persistence and maintaining one's values, not in immediate or absolute dominance.

2. A Marathon Runner Crossing the Finish Line
   A marathon runner trains tirelessly, enduring injuries, setbacks, and moments of self-doubt. During the race, they may not be the fastest, they may get cramps, they might even be tempted to take shortcuts, but they endure and finish with determination, overcoming their personal limits. Their victory isn't in winning the race but in persisting with integrity and achieving their goal.

   Key Takeaway: Just like Mahabali, the runner's achievement is a testament to the strength of character and persistence.

The story of Mahabali and Vamana teaches that true victory transcends material success. It is found in one's ability to persist with integrity, embrace humility, and navigate challenges with grace. Like Mahabali's yearly return during Onam, our victories—though humble—leave a legacy that lights the way for others.

Practical Exercises for the Lunar Mansion

1. Visualization: The Path of Victory

Close your eyes, imagine yourself walking along

a path that stretches toward the horizon. Along the way, you encounter challenges symbolized by fallen branches and steep hills. With each step, you overcome these obstacles, feeling your persistence growing stronger. As you reach the summit, a golden light bathes you in the warmth of success, symbolizing the fruits of your unwavering effort.

2. Journaling Prompt

Reflect on a goal or challenge where persistence paid off.

> What kept you going when things became difficult?
>
> How did the experience shape your confidence and determination?

Write about a current challenge or goal where persistence is required. What steps can you take today to move closer to success?

3. Action for the Day

Commit to an activity that requires patience and persistence. Whether it's completing a long-term project, resolving a lingering issue, or building a new habit, take deliberate steps forward with integrity and determination.

Advanced Exercises to Harness the Energy of Uttara Ashadha

a) Meditation with Sound

Purpose: Align with Uttara Ashadha's energy of

persistence and victory.

Meditate for 15 minutes to rhythmic marching cadences with distant trumpets. Feel the steady beats inspiring persistence and victory within you.

b) Connect to Nature

Purpose: Embody Uttara Ashadha's enduring and victorious essence.

Spend time observing a tall, sturdy tree or a mountain. Reflect on how their persistence through time and weather mirrors your ability to withstand challenges and grow stronger.

c) Perform a Service

Purpose: Encourage persistence and growth in others.

Help someone stay on track with their goals, whether by offering guidance, encouragement, or practical assistance. Your support can reinforce their determination and align you with Uttara Ashadha's energy. Do not expect anything in return.

"Persistence is the quiet march toward greatness; victory belongs to those who endure with integrity."

LUNAR MANSION 22: SHRAVANA

On the infinite canvas of the sky, the stars of Shravana —**Altair (Alpha Aquilae), Beta Aquilae, and Gamma Aquilae**—whisper tales of wisdom and discovery. Appearing like **three celestial footprints**, they remind us that every journey begins with listening. Governed by the **Moon** and anchored in the steadfast sign of **Capricorn** (ruled by **Saturn**), Shravana invites us to focus on the silence and hear the unspoken truths. Its spiritual theme, **"Listening and Learning"** unfolds a timeless cosmic message: **"Listen deeply. Wisdom unfolds in silence and the stories of others."**

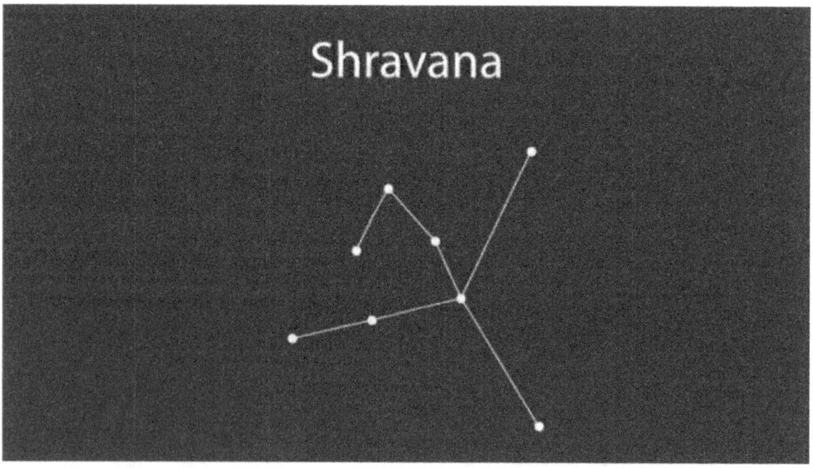

Image Source: https://popularvedicscience.com/astrology/shravana-nakshatra

---

The Story of Vishnu and the Ear of the Universe

Context

In Indian mythology, Lord Vishnu is a central figure in the Hindu trinity, known as the Preserver of the universe. His role is to maintain cosmic balance and harmony, often using wisdom, compassion, and subtlety rather than force. One of the 27 Nakshatras (lunar constellations), Shravana, symbolizes the art of deep listening and learning. It represents the ability to tune into the whispers of life—nature, people, and one's own soul—to gain wisdom and insight. This tale of Vishnu and the Ear of the Universe emphasizes the importance of listening not just with ears, but with the heart, to truly understand and grow.

The Story

The universe, when young, was a restless symphony. Chaos and creation collided, shaping a cosmos alive with untamed energy. Mortals and gods alike wandered through this maze, yearning for meaning, yet deaf to its quiet truths. In their longing, they turned to Lord Vishnu, the preserver of balance and wisdom.

"Lord Vishnu," they beseeched, bowing low before him, "you who guide the worlds, teach us to understand the whispers of the cosmos. The truths elude us, hidden in silence."

Vishnu's gaze which was deep as the ocean, softened. "The universe speaks," he said, his voice calm as the first light of dawn, "but only to those who listen—not with ears alone, but with hearts open to its rhythm. I will show you how."

To teach this, Vishnu descended to Earth, his celestial form cloaked in the guise of a wandering mendicant. Barefoot, he walked through dense forests where leaves murmured secrets, across deserts where winds carried ancient tales, and into cities alive with the hum of countless lives. He moved unseen, his presence gentle, his purpose clear: to help mortals hear what they were too busy to notice.

On his journey, he met three souls, each bothered by a question they could not answer.

The first was Keshav, a farmer, whose once-thriving fields now lay cracked and barren. Kneeling in the dust, he cried out to the heavens, "Why has the rain forsaken us? What sin have we committed?"

Vishnu approached, his steps light but deliberate. "Walk with me, Keshav," he said, his voice steady as the wind. "Listen—not to your despair, but to the earth beneath your feet."

Together, they wandered the fields. Vishnu gestured for Keshav to touch the soil, to feel its texture, its thirst. He pointed to the wind, carrying hints of distant moisture, and to the birds, whose flight patterns revealed the presence of underground springs. Slowly, Keshav began to see: the earth was not lifeless but waiting—for deeper roots, for careful exploration, for his attention.

"Do you hear it now?" Vishnu asked.

Keshav knelt, hands sifting through the soil, no longer crying out to the heavens but listening to the answers already whispered by the land.

In a bustling city, Vishnu found Sita, a merchant whose heart was heavy with worry. Her business teetered on the edge of collapse. "The market is cruel," she lamented. "It devours all I have worked for. Why does it turn its back on me?"

Vishnu invited her to sit by the marketplace. "Listen, Sita," he said, "not to your fears, but to the voices around you."

They sat in silence, the chaos of the market weaving stories into the air. Sita watched, her heart still. She noticed patterns she had ignored in her haste: the merchants who thrived were those who adapted, those who listened to their customers' needs and adjusted their offerings. She observed how they spoke, not to sell, but to connect. She observed the behavior of the buyers and how they responded to various elements in the market.

That evening, she returned to her shop with a new approach—not to compete, but to serve. The hum of the marketplace no longer overwhelmed her. Instead, it became a melody she could follow.

On the edge of a forest, Vishnu found Arjun, a warrior whose shoulders sagged with his guilt. His decisions in battle had cost lives, and their cries haunted him. "How can I bear what I have done?" he asked, his voice raw.

Vishnu led him to a still lake, its surface smooth as glass. "Listen, Arjun," he said, "not to your regrets, but to the water."

Arjun stared into the lake, his reflection trembling with

each ripple. As the breeze danced across the surface, he began to hear—not with his ears, but with his heart. The lake spoke of those who had come before him: warriors who had known loss, who had borne guilt, but who had also found redemption. He saw their sacrifices, their courage in the line of duty, and their ability to rise again.

The water, which was supposed to have a memory of its own, even listened to Arjun's story, not as condemnation, but as a chapter among many others. After a long time, he felt the burden of guilt lighten.

At dawn, Vishnu gathered the three by a mountain, its face carved with the immense shape of an ear. "This," Vishnu said, "is the Ear of the Universe. It hears all: the cries of the fields, the marketplace, and the battlefield. But it does not judge. It listens, understanding the stories woven into each voice."

As they gazed in awe, Vishnu placed his hand on the ear. It shimmered and dissolved into the sky, becoming a constellation that would forever remind the world to listen.

"The Ear of the Universe is not in the stars or mountains," Vishnu said, turning to them. "It is within you. When you listen deeply—to others, to the world, to your own heart—you carry its wisdom forward. In listening, you understand. In understanding, you heal."

The three returned to their lives transformed—not by epiphany, but by the realization that wisdom unfolds in the spaces where words fall silent and stories are truly heard. And above them, Shravana, the constellation of the Ear (hearing) glowed softly, a cosmic reminder of the power of deep listening.

Moral of the Story

Listening is the foundation of wisdom. By setting aside our biases, fears, and distractions, we can hear the truths that life whispers to us. Understanding begins not with speaking, but with silence and attention.

Modern-Day Relevance

In a world dominated by noise—social media chatter, endless notifications, and hurried conversations—Shravana's lesson is a call to reconnect with the art of listening.

> Professionally: Scenario: A manager hears complaints from their team but doesn't jump to conclusions. Instead, they actively listen, asking clarifying questions and understanding the root issues. This fosters trust and collaboration, ultimately resolving challenges with greater efficiency.
>
> Lesson from Shravana: Leaders who listen empower others and make informed decisions.
>
> Personally: Scenario: In relationships, people often listen only to respond, rather than to understand. Shravana teaches that setting aside distractions and truly hearing what loved ones share—whether joy or pain—strengthens bonds and deepens intimacy.
>
> Lesson from Shravana: Active listening shows care

and builds meaningful connections.

Spiritually: Scenario: Practicing mindfulness by listening to the rustling leaves, a flowing stream, or the beat of one's own heart brings clarity and inner peace.

Lesson from Shravana: Listening to life's subtle rhythms opens pathways to wisdom and serenity.

Shravana's energy reminds us that wisdom is always present, but it reveals itself only to those who truly listen.

Real-Life Analogies for New Seekers

1. A Mentor in a Crowded Classroom:

Imagine a teacher walking into a noisy classroom filled with students clamoring for attention. Instead of shouting to restore order, the teacher silently observes. By carefully listening to the conversations, they identify the students' concerns and confusion. Once they understand, the teacher offers precise guidance, turning chaos into clarity.

Key Takeaway: True leadership and problem-solving come from listening before acting.

2. A Gardener Tending to the Soil:

A gardener notices that their plants aren't thriving. Instead of rushing to add water or fertilizer, they kneel to feel the soil, check for pests, and observe the light patterns. By listening to what the garden is "telling" them, they realize the plants need better drainage, not more care.

> Key Takeaway: Listening to the needs of a situation, rather than assuming, leads to solutions that are both effective and harmonious.

The story of Vishnu and the Ear of the Universe reminds us that wisdom doesn't arise from talking or reacting, but from pausing to listen—deeply, patiently, and without judgment. In every noise, there is a truth waiting to be heard.

Practical Exercises for the Lunar Mansion

1. Visualization: The Whispering Stars

Close your eyes and imagine yourself lying under a vast night sky filled with countless stars. As you focus on the silence, you begin to hear gentle whispers of wisdom and guidance from the cosmos. These whispers illuminate the answers you've been seeking. Visualize yourself absorbing this wisdom and feeling a sense of peace and clarity.

2. Journaling Prompt

Reflect on a moment when listening deeply—whether to someone else, your intuition, or nature—brought you insight or understanding.

What did you learn from that experience?

How can you practice deeper listening in your life today?

Write about a question or challenge you're currently facing. What might the answer look like if you listened to your inner voice or observed the world around you more closely?

3. Action for the Day

Engage in a conversation where you focus entirely on listening without interrupting. If needed, you may simply say "Hmm" from time to time. Offer no platitudes, just listen and empathize. Whether it's a friend, a family member, or even your inner thoughts, let this act of listening deepen your understanding and strengthen your connections.

Advanced Exercises to Harness the Energy of Shravana

a) Meditation with Sound

Purpose: Align with Shravana's energy of listening and learning.

Meditate for 15 minutes to babbling brooks layered with echoing bird calls. Listen deeply, allowing the sounds to unfold wisdom and understanding.

b) Connect to Nature

Purpose: Embrace Shravana's essence of deep listening.

Spend time in a quiet natural setting, like a forest or near a stream. Focus on the subtle sounds around you—the rustle of leaves, birdsong, or the flow of water. Reflect on how much you can learn when you simply listen.

c) Perform a Service

Purpose: Share Shravana's energy of listening and

understanding.

Offer your time and full attention to someone who needs to be heard. Whether it's through a conversation, active support, or helping them clarify their thoughts, let your listening be a gift. Do not expect anything in return.

"To listen is to open the soul; wisdom flows not from speaking but listening to the silence between words."

LUNAR MANSION 23: DHANISHTA

In the sparkly spectacle of the cosmos, every star plays its part, and Dhanishta (**Alpha Delphini, Beta Delphini, Gamma Delphini, Delta Delphini**) resonates with **rhythm** and **prosperity**. Symbolized by the **drum** or **flute**, and powered by the energy of its ruler **Mars**, it calls us to attune ourselves to life's natural tempo, much like its corresponding zodiac signs, **Capricorn and Aquarius,** find their strength in **Saturn's** perseverance. This mansion teaches a profound truth: harmony is the foundation of abundance. **"Prosperity arises from attuning to life's rhythms. Dance in harmony with your purpose, with what you are naturally most suited for."** With each beat of the cosmic drum, Dhanishta invites us to move in sync with our inner melody.

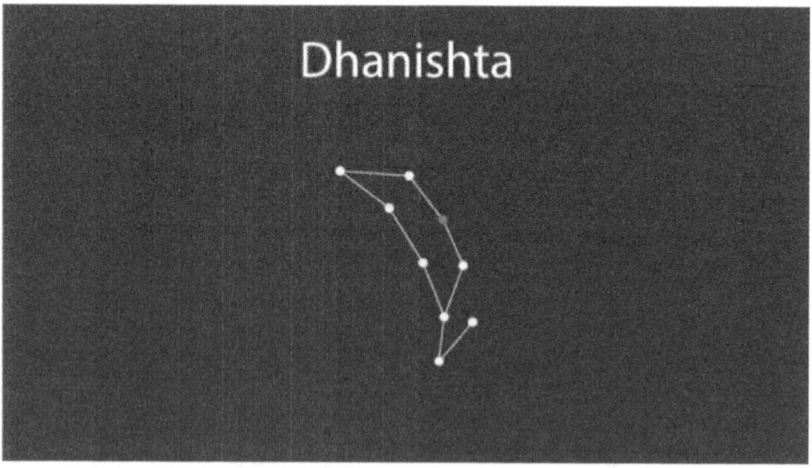

Image Source: https://popularvedicscience.com/astrology/dhanishtha-nakshatra

The Dance of Dhanishta: A Symphony of Prosperity

The Context

In Indian mythology, the universe is depicted as a vast symphony, where celestial beings orchestrate the forces of nature in perfect harmony. The *Vasus**, eight elemental deities representing earth, fire, water, wind, and other natural forces, are integral to maintaining this balance. They symbolize the rhythms of creation and prosperity.

The constellation of Dhanishta, tied to these divine beings, represents the interplay of rhythm and abundance. Its stories emphasize that prosperity is not achieved through dominance or isolation but through harmony and alignment with life's natural flow. This myth-inspired tale of the Vasus serves as a timeless reminder to attune ourselves to the rhythms of the world and collaborate for shared prosperity.

The Story

In the alchemy of the cosmic realms, the eight Vasus (Sky, Earth, Wind, Fire, Stars, Water, Sun, Moon) were revered as guardians of creation's rhythm. They wove an eternal symphony, their energies blending seamlessly to sustain the cosmos. Agni, the flame, brought warmth and vitality; Apas, the water, nourished life's flow; Anila, the wind, whispered renewal; and Prithvi, the earth, anchored it all. Together, they created a harmonious dance that sustained both the heavens and Earth.

For eons, their symphony was unbroken. The cycles of nature flourished, prosperity abounded, and life thrived.

But even in the heavens, discord has a way of seeping in. Prithvi, the earth Vasu, began to feel overshadowed. Her thoughts grew restless as she watched mortals worship Agni's fire in festivals and rituals.

"Without me, they would have no ground to stand on," she murmured, resentment creeping into her voice. "Yet, they only praise the brilliance of the flame."

Agni, too, grew arrogant with the adulation. "It is my fire that gives them life," he boasted, his flames flaring. "Without my warmth, all would wither."

The quiet murmur of discontent soon turned into heated arguments. Their quarrels echoed through the heavens, and the delicate balance began to falter. Rivers shrank, crops failed, and the winds turned wild. The once-perfect rhythm of creation unraveled, leaving both gods and mortals to suffer the loss.

Realizing the magnitude of their discord, the Vasus turned to Lord Shiva, the cosmic dancer who governs creation and destruction. They bowed before him, their celestial forms dimmed with shame.

"Lord of Rhythms," Prithvi said, her voice subdued, "our unity is broken. How can we restore the harmony we have lost?"

Shiva's gaze was sharp, his voice deep and resonant. "Harmony cannot be demanded; it must be rediscovered. Descend to the mortal realm. Live among those who dance to the rhythms of existence. Only then will you remember the song you have forgotten."

Reluctantly, the Vasus took mortal forms and descended

to Earth. Each gravitated toward a different rhythm of life, drawn by an unseen force. Prithvi walked among farmers, feeling their calloused hands coaxing life from the soil. Agni became a blacksmith, watching sparks fly as he shaped tools with precision. Apas flowed in rivers, witnessing fishermen cast their nets with patience. Anila traveled with wandering sages, discovering the power of breath and the whispers carried on the wind.

Weeks turned into months as they observed and learned. Yet, the true meaning of harmony still eluded them. Each Vasu remained immersed in their rhythm, unable to see beyond their own role.

One evening, their paths converged in a small village alive with celebration. The Festival of Rhythms was in full swing, a joyous tribute to nature's cycles. Drummers played beats that mirrored the heart's pulse, dancers moved like flowing rivers, and singers filled the air with melodies as light as the wind. Farmers stamped their feet in unison, and elders sang songs of gratitude for the harvest.

The Vasus stood apart, watching the villagers' effortless unity. Prithvi noticed how the farmers' steps matched the drummers' beats. Agni saw the blacksmiths crafting tools with the rhythm of the music. Apas felt the dancers flowing like water, and Anila marveled at how the singers' voices drifted on the wind. As they sat there for hours , admiring the festivities, a realization began to dawn.

It wasn't in their individual rhythms that the magic lay, but in how those rhythms intertwined. Each role was vital, yet incomplete on its own. Together, they created a symphony greater than the sum of its parts.

Compelled by this revelation, the Vasus stepped into the circle of dancers. At first, their movements were tentative, but as they synchronized with the villagers, their celestial essence began to reawaken. The earth felt fertile once more under Prithvi's touch. Rivers surged with life as Apas flowed. Agni's flames burned with vigor, and Anila's winds carried the scent of renewal. Prosperity touched the land in a manner that seemed everlasting.

As the final note of the festival faded, the villagers stood still, awestruck. Before them, the Vasus revealed their true forms, radiant and harmonious.

"You have reminded us of a truth we had forgotten," Prithvi said, her voice deep and filled with gratitude. "Prosperity arises not from supremacy, but from harmony—each rhythm attuned to the whole."

The Vasus ascended back to the heavens, their symphony restored. From that day on, the Festival of Rhythms became a sacred tradition, a reminder to mortals and gods alike that true prosperity lies in unity, in dancing to the rhythm of life, and in honoring the role each plays in the greater cosmic design.

Moral of the Story

True prosperity arises from harmony. When we align with life's rhythms and honor the interconnected roles we all play, we create balance, abundance, and joy.

Modern-Day Relevance

In our fragmented world, where competition often

overshadows collaboration, the story of the Vasus teaches us the importance of working in harmony to achieve shared prosperity.

Professionally: In today's workplace, collaboration is key. When team members recognize and respect each other's strengths and work together rhythmically, success follows. A competitive, discordant team, like the quarreling Vasus, disrupts productivity and harmony.

Personally: Families and relationships flourish when individuals honor each member's unique contributions. Harmony arises not from dominance but from mutual respect and alignment with shared goals.

Spiritually: Inner peace requires attuning to life's natural rhythms—balancing activity and rest, ambition and contentment. Practicing mindfulness, meditation, or spending time in nature can help you find your personal rhythm.

Dhanishta's energy reminds us that prosperity is not an individual pursuit. It is a symphony, a dance, and a rhythm we create together. By aligning with this flow, we thrive both as individuals and as a collective.

Real-Life Analogies for New Seekers

Analogy 1: A Successful Orchestra

Imagine an orchestra preparing for a performance. Each musician plays a different instrument, and no single one can carry the entire melody. If the violinist or percussionist tries to overshadow others, the music turns chaotic. However, when every musician plays in sync, respecting the conductor's rhythm, the result is a breathtaking symphony.

Lesson: True prosperity in work or relationships arises when individuals collaborate, each contributing their unique strengths while respecting the collective rhythm.

Analogy 2: A Flourishing Garden

Think of a thriving garden. Each element—sunlight, soil, water, and seeds—has a specific role and rhythm. Overwatering can drown the plants, and too much sunlight can scorch them. A gardener who observes and aligns with nature's timing, watering and nurturing plants in harmony with their needs, ensures a bountiful harvest.

Lesson: Personal growth and abundance come from respecting life's natural cycles, balancing effort with patience, and nurturing yourself and others in the right rhythm.

Dhanishta reminds us that prosperity is a collective dance of interconnected rhythms. By aligning with these rhythms, whether in teams, families, or within ourselves, we create harmony and abundance. Like the Vasus rediscovering their symphony, we too can thrive when we embrace the flow of life with balance and purpose.

Practical Exercises for the Lunar Mansion

1. Visualization: The Cosmic Drumbeat

Close your eyes and imagine yourself in a vast, open field under a starry sky. A rhythmic drumbeat begins to play, echoing the heartbeat of the cosmos. As you sway to the rhythm, feel yourself aligning with the natural flow of life. Visualize the beat syncing with your inner rhythms, guiding you toward prosperity and harmony.

2. Journaling Prompt

Reflect on the rhythms and patterns in your life.

> What routines or habits help you stay grounded and prosperous?
>
> Are there any rhythms you'd like to adjust to better align with your goals?

Write about a time when attuning to the right rhythm—whether in work, relationships, or self-care—helped you achieve balance or success.

3. Action for the Day

Engage in an activity that aligns with your personal rhythm, such as organizing your day to match your peak energy times or completing a task with focus and flow. Let this action enhance your productivity and joy. Remember, you don't have to be good at many things, you just have to build upon the one you are naturally suited to.

Advanced Exercises to Harness the Energy of Dhanishta

a) Meditation with Sound

Purpose: Align with Dhanishta's energy of prosperity and rhythm.

Meditate for 15 minutes to metallic cymbals in sync with soft drumbeats. Picture the sounds aligning your inner rhythms with the prosperity of life.

b) Connect to Nature

Purpose: Embody Dhanishta's rhythmic and prosperous essence.

Spend time observing natural rhythms, such as the waves of the ocean, the swaying of trees in the wind, or the footsteps of animals. Reflect on how these rhythms mirror the cycles of abundance and harmony in your life.

c) Perform a Service

Purpose: Share Dhanishta's energy of prosperity and rhythm with others.

Help someone organize or align their life's rhythms —whether it's assisting with their schedule, offering advice for balance, or helping them create a plan to achieve their goals. Do not expect anything in return.

"Prosperity dances to the rhythm of purpose; align your steps with the beats of your soul and you shall thrive."

LUNAR MANSION 24: SHATABHISHA

Shatabhisha (star **Gamma Aquarii**)—shines like a beacon of enigma, its symbol, **an empty circle,** whispering of the uncharted and the infinite. Known as the '**1000 Stars**' of healing, this nakshatra is under the guardianship of **Rahu (North Node)**, the cosmic prankster, and resonates with the zodiac sign of **Aquarius**, guided by the steadfast **Saturn**. Its spiritual theme weaves together **healing** and **mystery,** inviting us to journey into the unknown. Here, the cosmic message reminds us: **"Healing emerges from embracing the unknown. Let mystery inspire growth."**

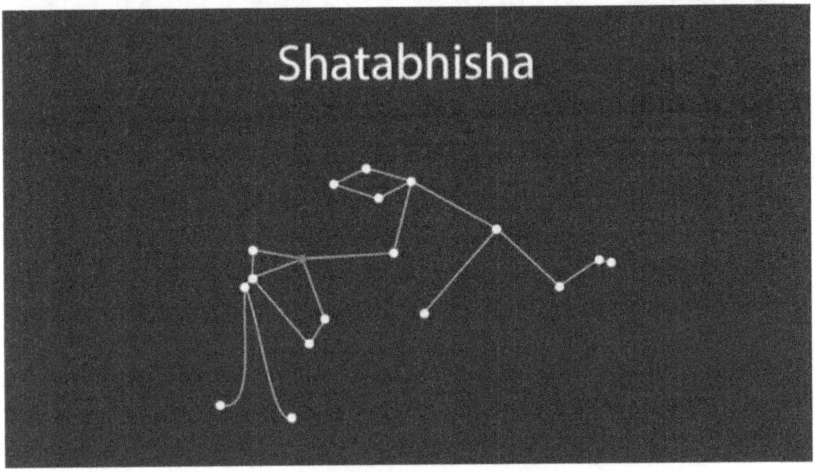

Image Source: https://popularvedicscience.com/astrology/shatabhisha-nakshatra

---

The Tale of Varuna and the Veil of Mysteries

Context for Readers

In Indian mythology, Varuna is a revered deity known

as the god of cosmic order, the oceans, and hidden truths. His dominion over the unseen makes him both a bringer of healing and a revealer of karmic justice. The Nakshatras, or lunar mansions, are celestial constellations that mark the moon's journey through the sky. Each Nakshatra represents a unique energy that influences life and guides spiritual growth.

The Shatabhisha Nakshatra is associated with healing and mysteries, inviting us to confront the unknown and trust its transformative power. The story of Varuna and Sanjana encapsulates these themes, teaching that true healing often emerges not from what we know, but from our willingness to embrace the unseen.

The Story

At the edge of the vast, unfathomable ocean, where the horizon blurred the line between the heavens and the waters, sat Varuna on his throne formed by rising waves. His gaze pierced the mist, the clouds and the veil of illusion, revealing truths buried deep within. To him came sailors, seekers, and wanderers, yearning for guidance or mercy, yet fearing his inscrutable judgment.

One day, a young healer named Sanjana arrived at the shore. Known across kingdoms for her uncanny ability to cure the incurable, Sanjana was celebrated, yet she carried a deep pain. Her younger sister, Mira, lay stricken by an illness that defied all her remedies. Sanjana had tried every tincture, incantation, and prayer, only to be met with failure. Desperation had driven her here, to Varuna's domain, where mortal pride dissolved before divine mystery.

Sanjana knelt by the shoreline, the salty wind stinging her eyes. "Lord Varuna," she called, her voice trembling with reverence and despair. "I have devoted my life to healing. I've healed kings and beggars, yet I cannot save my own sister. Tell me what I've missed. What lies beyond my reach?"

Varuna's gaze fell upon her, his eyes as deep and mercurial as the ocean itself. "Sanjana," he said, his voice calm yet weighty, "healing does not end at the boundaries of knowledge. Your remedies have touched her body, but not the depths of her being. Are you prepared to enter the unknown to find what you seek?"

Sanjana hesitated. Her mastery of healing had been her life's work, her identity. All her work was about evidence, and the unknown was a realm she had avoided—an abyss without the certainty of answers.

"What lies in the unknown?" she asked, her voice small.

Varuna gestured toward the horizon, where the sea stretched endlessly. "It holds truths you fear to face, shadows that cling to you like whispers in the dark. You must confront these to heal not just your sister, but yourself."

He led her to a secluded cove hidden by jagged rocks and dense mist. At its heart stood an archway of dark stone, veiled by a shimmering curtain of water that seemed alive. "This is the Veil of Mysteries," Varuna said. "Pass through it, and you will see what remains hidden. But beware: what you find may unsettle you."

Sanjana's heart pounded as she stepped forward, the mist

wrapping around her like a second skin. As she crossed the threshold, the world shifted. The air thickened, and the light dimmed until only shadows remained. From the darkness, voices emerged—soft, persistent murmurs that grew louder as she ventured deeper.

Fragments of memories played before her like fleeting dreams. Mira as a child, her laughter ringing through the air, her hand reaching out for Sanjana. And then, the laughter faded. Mira's outstretched hand remained unanswered as Sanjana turned away, engrossed in her studies, her ambitions.

"You sought perfection in mastery," a voice echoed, resonating through the void. "But at what cost? You healed others, yet neglected the one who needed you most. Her illness is not just of the body but of a heart left untended."

Sanjana fell to her knees, tears streaming down her face. Guilt rippled through her, sharp and cold. After their parents had passed, she had been so consumed by her pursuit of excellence that she had missed the silent suffering of the one she loved most. All her life, she had ignored her sibling who yearned for her love.

"How can I undo this?" she whispered into the darkness. "How can I heal her now?"

The voice softened, like a tide receding. "You cannot undo the past, but you can embrace it. Healing begins when you acknowledge what was broken and offer what you withheld: presence, love, connection. To heal is not to patch, but to mend, thread by thread."

As the words settled over her, the shadows began to shift,

revealing a dim light ahead. Sanjana rose and followed it, emerging from the Veil with a new understanding etched into her soul. Varuna awaited her by the shore.

"What did you see?" he asked, his tone both gentle and probing.

"I saw the roots of my sister's pain—and my own," Sanjana replied. "I sought to cure her body while ignoring the wounds I had left in her spirit."

Varuna handed her a chalice brimming with water that shimmered like liquid moonlight. "This is the water of mystery. It will not heal her alone, but it will guide her toward renewal if you walk the path with her."

Sanjana returned home and found Mira pale and frail, her breathing shallow. Kneeling beside her, Sanjana took her sister's hand and held it tightly, her voice trembling as she spoke.

"Mira, I'm sorry. I see now how I failed you, how my absence left you alone. But I'm here now. I'll walk with you through this, step by step."

She offered the chalice, and as Mira drank, a soft glow enveloped her. It was not a sudden miracle but a quiet awakening. Mira's eyes fluttered open, and for the first time in years, there was warmth in her gaze.

From that day forward, Sanjana's approach to healing transformed. She no longer sought mastery over ailments but instead embraced the mystery of each patient's unique journey. Her remedies touched more than the body; they reached into the spirit. And when patients asked her for the secret of her art, she would smile and say,

"Healing begins where knowledge ends—in the warm embrace of the unknown."

Moral of the Story

Healing is not always about solving a problem. It is about embracing the unknown, connecting with the root of the pain, and allowing growth to emerge. True healing often lies beyond logic, in the realms of love, forgiveness, and presence.

Modern-Day Relevance

In the modern world, we often seek certainty and control, especially in health and relationships. Varuna's tale reminds us that:

Professionally: In fields like medicine, education, or leadership, embracing the unknown can lead to breakthroughs. For instance, an educator might recognize that a struggling student's performance isn't due to lack of ability but underlying emotional challenges, addressing them with empathy rather than discipline.

Personally: In our fast-paced lives, relationships often suffer from lack of attention. Shatabhisha's story reminds us that healing broken bonds often requires acknowledging hidden emotions and offering love and forgiveness.

Spiritually: For spiritual seekers, uncertainty is often intimidating. Yet, practices like meditation, mindfulness, or trusting the flow of life encourage us to embrace the mysteries of existence, leading to profound transformation.

Shatabhisha's energy calls us to dive into the unknown, trust the process, and let mystery inspire the healing we seek.

Real-Life Analogies for New Seekers

Analogy 1: Seeking New Solutions in Medicine
Imagine a doctor treating a patient with an unexplained illness. Despite all tests and traditional treatments, the patient's condition remains unresolved. The doctor realizes that healing might require looking beyond clinical data—perhaps addressing emotional stress or environmental factors. By stepping into the unknown and embracing unconventional approaches like mindfulness or holistic care, the doctor helps the patient heal.

Lesson: Healing often requires stepping beyond established knowledge to explore deeper, less obvious causes.

Analogy 2: Rebuilding a Strained Relationship
Consider a person trying to mend a strained relationship with a loved one. Logical explanations and problem-solving haven't worked. The breakthrough comes when they open up emotionally, admit past mistakes, and listen without judgment. By embracing vulnerability and connecting on a deeper level, the relationship begins to heal.

Lesson: True healing in relationships requires stepping into uncomfortable truths and offering presence, love, and understanding.

Healing is not merely about solving problems; it is about confronting the unseen and allowing growth to unfold in unexpected ways. Whether in health, relationships, or self-discovery, Shatabhisha's energy teaches us to trust the unknown and find renewal in its embrace.

Practical Exercises for the Lunar Mansion

1. Visualization: The Veil of Mystery

Close your eyes and imagine standing before a shimmering curtain of light, representing the mysteries of life. As you step through the curtain, you find yourself surrounded by a celestial healing pool. Visualize the light from the pool bathing you, dissolving confusion and rejuvenating your spirit. Feel the healing energy seeping into every part of your being, unlocking answers hidden deep within.

2. Journaling Prompt

Reflect on a mystery or unanswered question in your life that intrigues or challenges you.

> How can embracing the unknown lead to growth or healing?
>
> What steps can you take to approach this mystery with curiosity rather than fear?

Write about a time when embracing uncertainty brought you unexpected insights or healing. What did you learn from that experience?

3. Action for the Day

Step out of your comfort zone today by exploring a topic or activity that feels unfamiliar or mysterious. Whether it's researching a new field, trying a different meditation technique, or exploring an artistic endeavor, let this act deepen your connection to Shatabhisha's energy.

Advanced Exercises to Harness the Energy of Shatabhisha

a) Meditation with Sound

Purpose: Align with Shatabhisha's energy of healing and mystery.

Meditate for 15 minutes to Tibetan singing bowls combined with faint water dripping. Envision the sounds healing your spirit and unveiling life's mysteries.

b) Connect to Nature

Purpose: Embrace Shatabhisha's enigmatic and restorative essence.

Spend time near a body of water under the night sky, reflecting on the vastness of the universe and the mysteries it holds. Let the interplay of water and starlight inspire you to embrace the unknown as a source of healing and growth.

c) Perform a Service

Purpose: Share Shatabhisha's energy of healing and transformation.

Offer support to someone navigating uncertainty or confusion. Whether it's providing a listening ear, sharing your own experiences, or guiding them through a reflective activity, your service can help them find clarity and healing. Do not expect anything in return.

"Healing begins in the unknown; the uncertainty you fear is the doorway to your growth."

LUNAR MANSION 25: PURVA BHADRAPADA

In the silence of the night sky, where **Alpha Pegasi (Markab)** and **Beta Pegasi (Scheat)** shimmer like celestial sentinels, the nakshatra of Purva Bhadrapada emerges as a realm of paradoxes—where sacrifice and surrender leads to transformation. Symbolized by **two crossed swords** or a **two-headed man** and governed by the wisdom of **Jupiter**, this nakshatra holds the cosmic tension of duality within its heart. Its spiritual essence is woven into the cusp of **Aquarius** and **Pisces**, realms shaped by the stern lessons of **Saturn** and the compassionate guidance of **Jupiter**. Here, the heavens whisper a profound truth: **"Sacrifice refines the spirit, paving the way for profound transformation."**

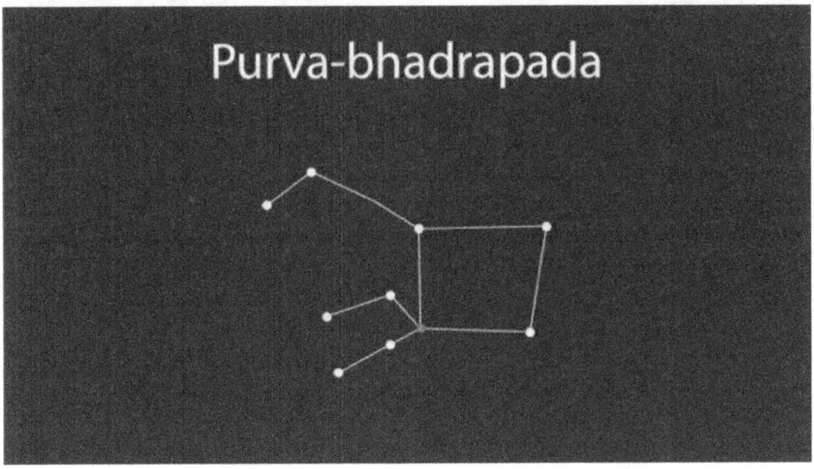

Image Source:https://popularvedicscience.com/ astrology/purva-bhadrapada-nakshatra

The Tale of Vritra and Indra: The Sacrifice for Transformation

Context for Readers

In Indian mythology, cosmic forces often battle to maintain balance in the universe. These conflicts, like those between the devas (gods) and asuras (demons or anti-gods or titans), symbolize the struggle between order and chaos, rather than good versus evil. Each side plays a vital role in the cosmic dance of creation, preservation, and transformation.

The story of Indra and Vritra embodies the theme of transformation through sacrifice, a powerful lesson in letting go of ego, control, or attachments for the greater good. For modern readers, this tale highlights how humility and surrender can lead to renewal and liberation, both for oneself and for others.

The Story

The land lay parched, cracked like an ancient scroll, whispering tales of desperation. Rivers had dried to barren beds, and the people's prayers for rain remained unanswered beneath an unrelenting sun. The devas, gathered in their heavenly council, bore the weight of Earth's suffering. At the center stood Indra, king of the gods, his brow furrowed with concern.

"This drought is not nature's doing," declared Agni, the god of fire. "The asura Vritra has seized the celestial rivers, coiling his vast body around their flow."

Indra clenched his fists. Vritra was no mere asura;

his strength rivaled the heavens, and his resolve was unyielding. Yet the plight of the earth demanded action. "I will face him," Indra said, his voice resolute. "Even if it means my end."

Clad in his divine armor and wielding the thunderbolt Vajra, Indra descended to the jagged mountains where Vritra dwelled. The sight was daunting: Vritra's colossal form encircled the rivers, his scales gleaming obsidian under the faint light, and his eyes burned with ancient defiance.

"Why have you come, Indra?" Vritra's voice rumbled, the mountains trembling under its weight. "Do you think your thunderbolt can break me?"

"I come for the waters," Indra replied, stepping forward. "The earth suffers. Release them, or face my wrath."

Vritra's laughter reverberated through the valley. "The waters are mine now. If you seek them, prove your worth."

The battle that ensued was a ruckus of chaos. Thunder and shadow clashed, each strike lighting the sky as if day and night fought for dominion. But Vritra's strength was insurmountable. Each blow from Indra's thunderbolt dissipated against the asura's coiled might, leaving the god bloodied and worn.

Gasping for breath, Indra lowered his weapon. He realized brute force would not defeat this foe. "What is it you truly want, Vritra?" he asked, his voice steady despite his exhaustion.

The asura paused, his massive form coiling tighter as if

bracing against an unseen burden. "What do I want?" he echoed, his voice carrying an unexpected sorrow. "I want freedom—from this endless cycle of conflict. My strength binds me, a curse that compels me to resist and destroy."

Indra's heart stirred with understanding. In Vritra's defiance, he saw not malice but a weary spirit trapped in its role. The asura was a force of resistance, a necessary shadow to the cosmic light, yet one that bore the weight of its destiny alone.

At that moment, Indra made a choice. Casting the Vajra aside, he stepped forward and knelt before Vritra. "If freedom is what you seek, then take it from me. Let my life release you from your burden. In return, grant the rivers their flow."

The heavens grew silent, as if holding their breath. Vritra's fiery eyes softened. "Would you sacrifice yourself for them?" he asked, his voice trembling.

"A king's duty is to his people," Indra replied. "If my life can restore balance, then so be it."

For a long moment, Vritra gazed at the king of gods kneeling before him. Slowly, his coils loosened, and the rivers began to flow once more. Water surged down the mountains, quenching the earth's thirst. Rain clouds gathered, and life returned to the parched lands below.

Vritra's immense form began to dissolve into a shimmering mist. "You have shown me the strength that lies in surrender, Indra," he said, his voice now a gentle whisper. "At last, the curse is lifted. I was bound until someone of great authority surrendered before me, not driven by their fear, but by the selflessness of their true sacrifice. Now, I am free because of your virtue."

As his spirit rose to merge with the clouds, Indra stood transformed. The weight of the thunderbolt in his hand now felt different—a symbol not of dominance but of humility. In his adversary's struggle, he had found a reflection of his own pride and a lesson in sacrifice.

From that day forward, Indra ruled with a renewed heart. He understood that power was not in wielding might but in recognizing the humanity—or divinity—even within his greatest foes. The rains that fell were no longer a mere boon of his thunderbolt but a reminder of the transformation that sacrifice could bring.

And so, the earth flourished once more, its rivers flowing freely, nourished not just by rain but by the unyielding spirit of sacrifice and the profound transformation it inspired.

Moral of the Story

Sacrifice is not an act of weakness but a path to transformation. True strength lies in the willingness to let go—for others, for balance, and for the greater good. Through sacrifice, we transcend our limitations and create space for renewal.

Modern-Day Relevance

In our world, the idea of sacrifice is often misunderstood as loss or defeat. But Purva Bhadrapada's energy reminds us that through sacrifice, we achieve growth, transformation, and a deeper connection to life's purpose.

Professionally: Leaders who prioritize the well-being of their team or organization often foster trust and innovation. For example, stepping aside to let someone else lead a project can empower others and strengthen the team as a whole.

Personally: In relationships, letting go of grudges or ego in a conflict can transform dynamics, paving the way for deeper harmony and mutual respect.

Spiritually: Sacrificing control over external circumstances —accepting the unpredictable nature of life—can lead to profound inner peace and spiritual awakening.

The story of Vritra and Indra shows that true strength lies in sacrifice, not dominance. When we surrender our ego or attachments for a greater cause, we pave the way for transformation, not just in ourselves but in the world around us.

Real-Life Analogies for the New Seekers

1. Real-Life Analogy 1: The Parent's Sacrifice

A parent often sacrifices personal comforts—time, energy, and resources—for the well-being of their children. This act of love and selflessness shapes the child's future while possibly transforming the parent into a more patient, understanding, and compassionate individual.

Key Takeaway: Like Indra, parents embody the strength to give up their own desires, resulting in deeper fulfillment and growth for both themselves and their children.

2. Real-Life Analogy 2: A Team Leader's Decision

Imagine a manager facing a challenging project deadline. To ensure the team's morale and well-being, they work overtime and forgo personal recognition, focusing instead on empowering their team members. The team succeeds because the leader sacrificed personal gains for collective success.

Key Takeaway: True leadership, like Indra's selfless act, comes not from wielding authority but from sacrificing for the greater good, fostering trust and transformation.

Practical Exercises for the Lunar Mansion

1. Visualization: The Flame of Sacrifice

Close your eyes and imagine yourself standing in front of a sacred fire. This flame represents transformation through sacrifice. Visualize yourself offering into the fire something you're not yet ready to release but you intend to—whether it's a fear, an attachment, or a limiting belief. As the flames consume it, feel a sense of lightness and renewal, as though space has been cleared for deeper growth.

2. Journaling Prompt

Reflect on an area of your life where letting go or sacrificing something could bring growth or transformation.

> What are you holding onto, and why?
>
> How can releasing it create space for new opportunities?

Write about a time when making a sacrifice led to significant personal or spiritual growth. How did it change you?

3. Action for the Day

Identify one small thing you can release today—a habit, an item, or even a moment of your time to help someone else. Let this act of letting go serve as a reminder of Purva Bhadrapada's transformative energy.

Advanced Exercises to Harness the Energy of Purva Bhadrapada

a) Meditation with Sound

Purpose: Connect with Purva Bhadrapada's energy of transformation through sacrifice.

Meditate for 15 minutes to the crackling of burning embers. Let the fire dissolve limitations, creating space for profound transformation.

b) Connect to Nature

Purpose: Embody Purva Bhadrapada's essence of transformative sacrifice.

Spend time near a bonfire or under a setting sun, observing how the fire or fading light symbolizes the cycles of release and renewal. Reflect on the beauty of endings as precursors to beginnings.

c) Perform a Service

Purpose: Share Purva Bhadrapada's transformative energy through selflessness.

Volunteer with a substantial amount of time or valuable resources for a cause that benefits others, such as helping at a shelter, donating to a charity, or offering support to someone in need. Let this act reflect the power of sacrifice to create positive change. Do not expect anything in return.

"Sacrifice is the alchemy of the soul, turning the ordinary into the eternal."

LUNAR MANSION 26: UTTARA BHADRAPADA

Gamma Pegasi (Algenib) and Alpha Andromedae (Alpheratz) shimmer at night to form Uttara Bhadrapada. **Saturn**, the planetary lord, casts its grounding influence over this realm, symbolized by **twins** or **dualistic imagery**—a reflection of balance between the material and spiritual. Nestled in the **Piscean** waters ruled by **Jupiter**, this mansion tells seekers: **"True stability comes from inner depth. Anchor yourself in spirit, not circumstance."** Here begins a journey, not into the external, but into the limitless sanctuary within.

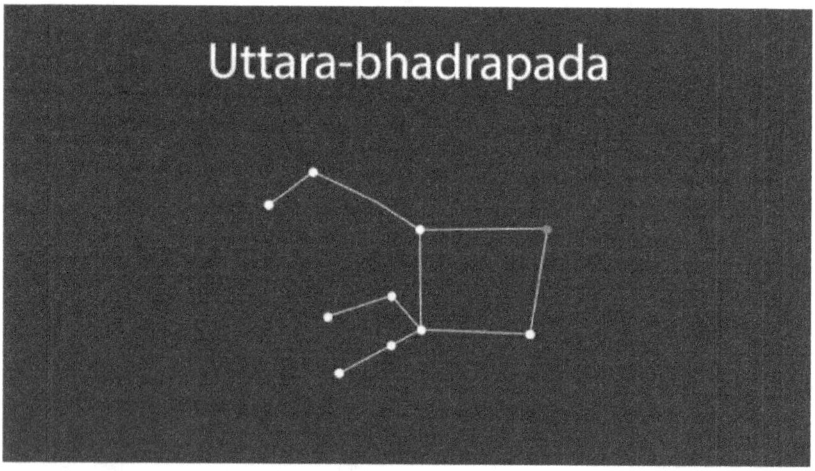

Image Source:https://popularvedicscience.com/astrology/uttara-bhadrapada-nakshatra

---

The Tale of *Shesha: The Eternal Balance**

Context for Readers

In Indian mythology, Shesha, the cosmic serpent,

embodies the ultimate symbol of stability and spiritual depth. Depicted as an endless serpent with a thousand radiant heads, Shesha supports the universe on his coils, signifying balance and tranquility amidst the chaos of creation. His journey teaches us that stability doesn't come from controlling external circumstances but from anchoring ourselves in inner peace and spiritual understanding.

This myth-inspired story relates to the 26th lunar mansion, Uttara Bhadrapada, which represents the energy of profound stability and spiritual depth. It invites us to transcend fleeting attachments and find true balance within ourselves.

The Story

Eons ago, in the nascent days of creation, the universe pulsed with unbridled chaos. Stars flared and dimmed, the Earth groaned under its own struggles to acquire a spherical shape, and the celestial spheres spun wildly, as if searching for their place. The gods looked upon this tumult with concern, but Vishnu, the Preserver, stood serene amid the disorder, his gaze fixed on the eternal.

"A sense of stability must be established," Vishnu declared, "and there is only one creature capable of bearing this burden."

He turned to Shesha, his devoted companion in the form of a serpent, whose countless heads shimmered with the brilliance of the cosmos. "Shesha," Vishnu said, "you are destined to uphold the universe. But to carry such a weight, you must first discover your own true essence. Go and travel across creation. Face its trials. Only then will you find the depths that anchor all things."

Shesha bowed deeply, his serpentine form coiling in reverence. "As you command, my lord. I shall seek my true internal essence."

His journey began in the mortal realm, where his immense presence shook the very fabric of the Earth. Mountains fractured, rivers shifted their courses, and the wind roared in protest. Mortals fled, their hearts unable to comprehend the vastness of the alien being before them. But Shesha paid them no mind; his focus was on the task Vishnu had set before him.

He sought out the elements, hoping they would teach him the secret of stability. First, he descended into the heart of a volcano. The molten core raged around him, its heat scorching even his celestial form. "Teach me stability," Shesha demanded.

The volcano erupted in laughter, its fiery rivers of lava surging wildly. "Stability is not in standing unmoved," it roared. "It is in flowing with purpose, unbroken by resistance."

Puzzled but undeterred, Shesha dove into the ocean's depths. The crushing weight of the water pressed against him, and the cold seeped into his very being. "Teach me stability," he implored.

The ocean's voice was a deep, echoing whisper. "Stability is not found in depth alone," it said. "It lies in embracing the light above, even as you sink into the dark."

Shesha's search continued. He traveled to the farthest reaches of the cosmos, where stars were born and galaxies collided. He faced storms of stardust and the silence of voids. Yet no matter where he went, the secret of stability eluded him. Exhausted by his failure, Shesha returned to Vishnu, his multiple heads bowed low.

"My lord," he said, his voice faint with weariness, "I have searched the fire, the water, and the stars themselves. Yet I am no closer to understanding my true essence or the inner stability you seek."

Vishnu acknowledged him with a gentle smile and gestured to a tranquil lake nearby. Its surface was so still that it mirrored the heavens perfectly. "Enter its waters," Vishnu said. "But this time, do not seek. *Simply be.*"

Reluctantly, Shesha lowered himself into the lake. The cool water embraced him, and for the first time, he did not strive to understand or conquer. He let his countless thoughts drift, his massive form settling into the stillness of the water. Time seemed to dissolve. The ripples he created merged back into the surface, leaving no trace of disturbance.

As he rested there for many years, a profound realization emerged, not in a sudden epiphany but as a gentle unfolding, like a flower blooming in the morning light. Stability, Shesha understood, was not about resisting the weight of the worldly concerns but in how one bore it. The weight itself was not the burden—it was his resistance to it that made it so.

"To anchor the universe," he murmured, "I must first anchor myself. The depth I seek is within."

When Shesha emerged from the lake after hundreds of years, his form radiated a serenity that seemed to calm the very air around him. Vishnu approached, his eyes filled with quiet pride. "You have found the answer, Shesha," he said. "True stability comes from inner depth. Anchor yourself in spirit, not in circumstance."

Shesha nodded, his many heads bowing in unison. As his understanding deepened, so did his form. His coils stretched across the cosmos, becoming the bedrock upon which creation rested. He supported the Earth, the stars, and the heavens, his calm presence a constant reminder of the balance he had found.

Many millennia passed, and mortals gazed at the night sky, marveling at the Milky Way, the celestial river formed by Shesha's luminous scales. What they could not see was the eternal meditation that anchored him, a stillness so profound that it upheld the weight of the universe itself. Shesha's stability was not a triumph over chaos but a harmonious embrace of all that was, is, and will be—rooted in the unshakable core within him.

Moral of the Story

True stability is not about controlling the chaos around us but finding the stillness within. When we anchor ourselves in spiritual depth and inner peace, we can carry the weight of the world without faltering.

Modern-Day Relevance

In today's world, we often seek stability in external circumstances—jobs, relationships, or material possessions—only to find that they are transient and unreliable. Shesha's story reminds us that:

Professional: A leader facing a challenging project deadline might feel overwhelmed by shifting circumstances. Instead of reacting to external pressures, focusing on inner clarity and thoughtful planning helps them guide their team effectively, ensuring stability and success.

Personal: In relationships, emotional stability doesn't come from trying to control others' actions. Instead, cultivating self-awareness and inner strength fosters resilience, allowing relationships to thrive amidst challenges.

Spiritual: Life's unpredictability often leads to anxiety or stress. Shesha's story reminds us that by grounding ourselves in spiritual depth—through meditation, mindfulness, or introspection—we can find peace that isn't tied to external circumstances.

Through Shesha's journey, Uttara Bhadrapada's wisdom teaches us that the foundation of stability lies within us. By finding inner depth and anchoring ourselves in spiritual practices, we can gracefully bear life's challenges, becoming a source of balance for ourselves and others.

Real-Life Analogies for the New Seekers

1. The Calm Captain in a Storm:

Imagine a ship's captain steering through a raging storm. While the waves crash and the winds howl, the captain's calm demeanor ensures the crew's safety. If the captain were to panic, the chaos would overwhelm the ship. Shesha's story mirrors this lesson: true stability doesn't come from controlling the storm but from maintaining inner calm amidst it.

Key Takeaway: In turbulent times—whether a workplace crisis or personal upheaval—calmness and inner clarity are the anchors that guide us through.

---

2. A Deep-Rooted Tree:

Picture a tree standing firm during a hurricane. Its branches sway wildly, but its deeply rooted trunk remains unshaken. The tree doesn't resist the wind but bends gracefully, its stability coming from its connection to the earth below. Similarly, Shesha discovers that true stability arises not from external forces but from the depth and stillness within.

Key Takeaway: Like the tree, we must cultivate strong roots—spiritual practices, self-awareness, and inner peace—to stay grounded amidst life's uncertainties.

Practical Exercises for the Lunar Mansion

1. Visualization: The Calm Depths

Close your eyes and imagine yourself descending into a deep, tranquil lake. As you dive deeper, the water becomes still and quiet, symbolizing inner stability and spiritual depth. Visualize yourself reaching the bottom, where a glowing pearl awaits

—a symbol of your inner wisdom and spiritual foundation. Hold the pearl and feel its steady, grounding energy anchoring you in peace.

2. Journaling Prompt

Reflect on the areas of your life where you feel stable and grounded.

> What contributes to this sense of stability?
>
> How can you deepen this foundation to weather life's uncertainties?

Write about a time when remaining calm and centered helped you navigate a challenge. How did this experience deepen your spiritual or personal strength?

3. Action for the Day

Dedicate time to a grounding practice today, such as meditation, journaling, or organizing your living space. Focus on creating a sense of calm and stability within yourself and your environment.

Advanced Exercises to Harness the Energy of Uttara Bhadrapada

a) Meditation with Sound

> Purpose: Align with Uttara Bhadrapada's energy of stability and spiritual depth.
>
> Meditate for 15 minutes to deep resonant bells with gong echoes. Feel the vibrations stabilizing your inner world and connecting you to spiritual depth.

b) Connect to Nature

Purpose: Embrace Uttara Bhadrapada's grounding and reflective essence.

Spend time near a still body of water, such as a lake or a quiet pond. Observe the water's calm surface and its ability to reflect clearly, symbolizing the stability and clarity that come from inner depth.

c) Perform a Service

Purpose: Share Uttara Bhadrapada's grounding energy with others.

Offer guidance or reassurance to someone feeling overwhelmed or shaken by life. Whether through a calming conversation, practical advice, or simply being a steady presence, help them find their footing. Do not expect anything in return.

"Stability is not the absence of storms but the depth of your spirit's anchor."

LUNAR MANSION 27: REVATI

As the final step of this 27 day journey, the singular star **Zeta Piscium** marks Revati, and beckons like a gentle tide pulling one toward the vast ocean of eternity. Its symbol, a **fish** or **drum**, whispers of rhythms long heard—those of journeys completed and destinies fulfilled. Governed by **Mercury** and nestled in the zodiac of **Pisces** under **Jupiter's** benevolent gaze, this mansion is both an ending and a beginning.

Spiritual Theme: Nourishing and protecting those standing at the threshold of **completion** and **liberation.**

Cosmic Message: "Completion is not an end but a *sacred transition**. True nourishment can be offered by guiding others toward liberation, providing protection and wisdom along the way, as they prepare to merge with the infinite."

Revati teaches us that the act of protection is not only about shelter but about preparing souls to let go. It whispers that every journey, no matter how vast, must one day dissolve into the infinite.

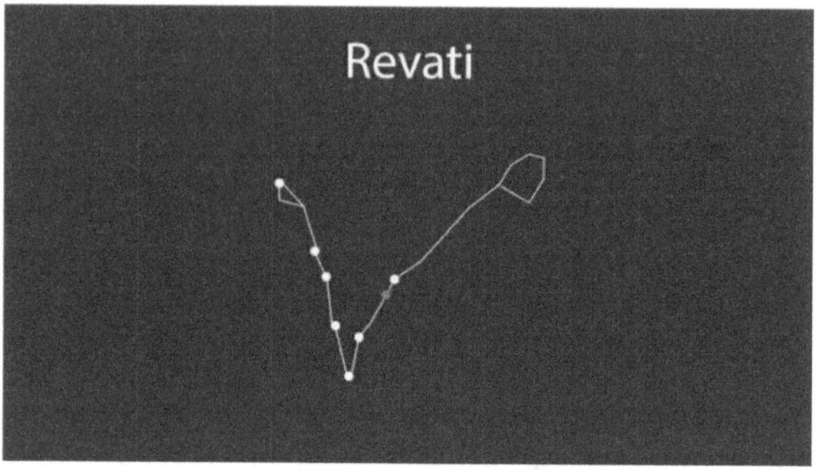

Image source: https://popularvedicscience.com/astrology/revati-nakshatra

The Tale of Revati: The Song of Completion

Context for Readers

As per Vedic Astrology, each Nakshatra symbolizes unique cosmic energies and life lessons, forming a celestial guide for spiritual growth. The 27th and final Nakshatra, Revati, represents completion and transcendence, akin to the final stage of a journey where we merge with something greater. This Nakshatra invites us to reflect on the beauty of endings—not as losses but as openings to infinite possibilities.

The story of Revati, a divine princess, encapsulates this theme by illustrating the harmony between earthly experiences and cosmic cycles. It teaches us to let go of attachments and embrace the flow of time, resonating with anyone navigating transitions or closure in their own lives.

The Story

Long ago, in an age when the divine and mortal realms thrived together, there was a king named Kakudmi. His kingdom flourished under his wise rule, a land of harmony and abundance. Yet, amidst this prosperity, Kakudmi was troubled by a fatherly responsibility. His only daughter, Revati, was a being of unparalleled grace and beauty, her presence akin to a soothing melody that calmed even the most troubled hearts. Her laughter, soft and resonant, lingered like the echo of temple bells.

Many suitors came, drawn by tales of her virtues, but Kakudmi found none worthy. He sought perfection for his daughter—a partner who could match her brilliance and carry her spirit forward. But the more he searched, the more elusive his ideal became.

One day, Kakudmi decided to seek the wisdom of Brahma, the Creator, believing the divine could guide him where mortal wisdom failed. With Revati beside him, he ascended to Brahmaloka, the celestial abode of Brahma.

Upon arrival, they found Brahma enraptured in a symphony played by the Gandharvas, the celestial musicians. The music resonated with the pulse of creation itself, each note weaving threads of joy. Kakudmi, captivated yet mindful of his purpose, waited patiently. Beside him, Revati closed her eyes, her breath synchronizing with the rhythm, her soul attuned to the cosmic melody.

When Brahma turned his attention to them, Kakudmi bowed deeply. “O Creator, my daughter’s beauty and virtue surpass mortal bounds. I seek your guidance to find her an equal, a husband who can match her essence."

Brahma acknowledged him with a knowing smile. "Kakudmi, you have journeyed far, yet you do not see what lies before you. In your pursuit of perfection, you have forgotten the passage of time."

Confused, Kakudmi asked, "What do you mean, my lord?"

Brahma's voice softened, like a teacher guiding an eager student. "Time here flows differently than on Earth. While you have lingered in this realm, listening to the eternal symphony, countless ages have passed in your world. The kingdom you ruled, the suitors you sought—they are but echoes now, dissolved into the currents of time."

Kakudmi's heart sank. "If all that I knew is gone, what remains for us?"

Brahma gestured toward Revati, whose face, though serene, held a quiet sadness. "Completion is not about clinging to what was, but embracing what is to come. Revati's destiny is not bound to the past but to a purpose greater than herself. She is meant for *Balarama*[*], the brother of Krishna. Their union will guide others toward liberation, bridging worlds as they prepare to merge with the infinite."

The words stirred something within Revati, though she did not fully grasp their meaning. She felt an unfamiliar pull, as though her spirit was being called toward an unseen horizon.

Returning to Earth, Kakudmi and Revati found

themselves in a world transformed. Forests had grown over once-familiar landscapes, rivers had carved new paths, and the air buzzed with the energy of a new era. They heard tales of Krishna and Balarama, divine beings who walked among mortals, and Kakudmi resolved to find them.

When they finally stood before Balarama, he looked at Revati with a gaze that seemed to pierce through time. "I have heard your song," he said, his voice steady and warm. "It has traveled through ages to reach me."

In that moment, Revati felt an undeniable connection. Not a spark of romance, but a deep resonance, as if her soul had found its missing part. Their union was not an ordinary marriage but a convergence of energies. Together, Revati's deep wisdom and Balarama's enormous strength became a force of balance and guidance. They nurtured their people, offering protection and wisdom, leading them toward inner peace and understanding.

Years passed. As their earthly duties drew to a close, Revati often sat by a river, watching its waters flow endlessly toward the sea. She marveled at its journey, unending yet whole, its purpose fulfilled in its merging. One evening, as twilight painted the sky in hues of pink, she turned to Balarama. "The river knows no fear of the ocean. It flows, not as an end, but as a sacred transition."

Balarama nodded, his hand resting on hers. "And so do we."

The river glowed faintly as if responding to her words. Revati stood at its edge, her heart light, her spirit unbound. Stepping into the water, she felt it embrace her like an old friend. The world around her shimmered, dissolving into a golden light. As she merged with the infinite, the river carried her essence forward, a melody that would linger in the hearts of those she had touched.

Completion, after all, was not an end but a sacred passage —a journey into eternity.

Moral of the Story

Completion is not about clinging to the past or fearing the end. It is about letting go and merging with the infinite flow of existence. True fulfillment comes when we transcend the limits of time and self, embracing what lies beyond.

Modern-Day Relevance

1. Professionally:

   Scenario: A person retiring after decades of work might feel a void, fearing the loss of identity tied to their career.

   Revati's Lesson: See retirement not as the end of productivity but as a chance to contribute differently—mentoring others, pursuing hobbies, or dedicating time to causes they're passionate about. Completion paves the way for new beginnings.

2. Personally:

   Scenario: Moving on from a long-term relationship or life phase can evoke grief and uncertainty.

Revati's Lesson: Letting go of attachments allows space for self-growth and new relationships that align with who you are becoming. Trust the flow of life to guide you to greater harmony.

3. Spiritually:

Scenario: Contemplating mortality can feel overwhelming.

Revati's Lesson: Embrace impermanence as a natural part of existence. Just as Revati merges with the infinite, spiritual practices like meditation and gratitude help us focus on eternal truths, fostering peace and acceptance.

Real-Life Analogies for the new seekers:

1. Graduation Day:

Imagine a student completing their studies and graduating. The day is filled with both nostalgia for the past and excitement for the future. The student must let go of the college fun, the comfort of the company of friends and the familiar routine of school to embrace the opportunities awaiting them in the world. Like Revati merging with the infinite, the student transitions from one phase of life to another, carrying forward lessons and experiences.

Key Takeaway: The ending of a chapter is not a loss but a gateway to greater horizons.

2. A River Meeting the Ocean:

Picture a river flowing steadily toward the ocean.

Along its journey, the river serves many purposes—quenching thirst, nourishing crops, and sustaining life. Yet, when it meets the vastness of the ocean, it doesn't resist; it merges, becoming part of something boundless. This mirrors Revati's transcendence as she embraces the infinite.

Key Takeaway: Completion means fulfilling one's purpose and moving on to a greater existence.

Revati's story and cosmic message remind us that endings are not defeats but opportunities for transcendence. By letting go, we align ourselves with the infinite flow of life, discovering renewal and purpose in every transition.

Practical Exercises for the Lunar Mansion

1. Visualization: The Infinite Horizon

Close your eyes and imagine yourself walking along a tranquil path that leads to the edge of a vast ocean. As you reach the shore, the sun sets, merging the sea and sky in a brilliant glow of gold and purple. Visualize yourself stepping into the water, feeling its embrace dissolve your worries and merge you with the infinite. Feel a deep sense of completion, as though all aspects of your journey have aligned.

2. Journaling Prompt

Reflect on an area of your life where you've recently reached a sense of completion or fulfillment.

What lessons or experiences have shaped this

journey?

How can you use these insights to inspire your next steps?

Write about a time when letting go of something brought you closer to a sense of peace and transcendence. What did this experience teach you about endings and beginnings?

3. Action for the Day

Perform an act of closure or completion today. Finish a task you've been putting off, reach out to resolve a lingering conflict, or let go of something that no longer serves you. Celebrate this act as a step toward transcendence and renewal.

Advanced Exercises to Harness the Energy of Revati

a) Meditation with Sound

Purpose: Align with Revati's energy of completion and transcendence.

Meditate for 15 minutes to a flowing orchestral symphony with harp and cello. Imagine the harmonious sounds merging your essence with the infinite, bringing transcendence.

b) Connect to Nature

Purpose: Embrace Revati's essence of merging and letting go.

Spend time at the edge of a body of water during sunrise or sunset. Reflect on how the water meets the horizon, symbolizing the merging of finite and infinite, and let this inspire a sense of peace and unity within you.

c) Perform a Service

Purpose: Help someone else achieve a sense of closure or peace.

Assist someone in completing a project, resolving a lingering issue, or letting go of a past burden. Your act of service will embody Revati's theme of transcendence and harmony. Do not expect anything in return.

"Completion is the river meeting the ocean, a journey not to an end but to infinite belonging."

EPILOGUE

As you close the final pages of this book, the journey doesn't end—it transforms. The myth-inspired stories of the 27 lunar mansions, the cosmic messages and the practices are not merely lessons to be read; they are seeds planted within your consciousness. Like the moon's phases, your understanding and growth will wax and wane, but always with the promise of renewal and discovery.

The Nakshatras have guided sages, seekers, and wanderers for millennia, illuminating the path of life's cycles—beginnings, transformations, and completions. They have whispered truths about the cosmos and the self, bridging the infinite vastness of the universe with the intimate inner world of the soul. Their wisdom transcends time and culture, speaking directly to the heart of human existence.

In the fast-paced, unpredictable world we inhabit today, their messages are more relevant than ever. They remind us to slow down, to reflect, and to realign with the rhythms of life and the universe. They challenge us to see life not as a series of obstacles to overcome but as a dance of energies to embrace, a story to live fully.

As you move forward, consider this: the power of the Nakshatras lies not in their celestial positions but in how they inspire you to navigate your life. Every action you take, every reflection you embrace, every connection you nurture becomes a constellation within—guiding you, empowering you, and revealing the infinite possibilities of your being.

Let the Nakshatras become your companions, not just in the skies but in your heart. Trust their guidance as you chart your path toward clarity, strength, and transformation. And when life feels uncertain, remember the stars are always shining—sometimes hidden by clouds, but never extinguished.

This is your journey, your constellation to create. Step into it with courage, curiosity, and grace.

GREY PAGES (GLOSSARY & APPENDIX)

Glossary:

1. **Agni:** is the Vedic god of fire, representing transformation, purification, and the link between the earthly and the divine. As the messenger of the gods, he carries offerings to the heavens and symbolizes energy, passion, and renewal in both spiritual and material realms.
2. **Amrita (uhm-ree-tah)**: In Hindu mythology, the nectar of immortality sought by gods and celestial beings, symbolizing ultimate wisdom or enlightenment.
3. **Ashwini Kumaras (ush-win-ee koo-mah-ras)**: Twin celestial healers in Hindu mythology associated with vitality and healing, connected to the Ashwini Nakshatra.
4. **Asura (uh-soo-rah)**: Powerful beings in Hindu mythology, often portrayed as antagonists of the Devas (gods). They symbolize ego, ambition, and material desires.
5. **Ayodhya (ah-yo-dhya)**: The ancient city associated with Lord Rama, a central figure in the Hindu epic Ramayana.
6. **Balarama**: As per Vedic mythology, Balarama is the elder brother of Krishna and a key figure in many Indian epics. Known for his immense strength and his association with agriculture and farming, he is often depicted with a plough (hala) as his weapon. Balarama symbolizes duty, strength, and a life lived in harmony with nature.
7. **Betelgeuse**: A bright red star in the constellation Orion, associated with the Ardra Nakshatra, symbolizing transformation through chaos.
8. **Brahma (bruh-mah)**: The creator god in the Hindu trinity, responsible for bringing the universe into existence. Brahma symbolizes the creative force.
9. **Brihaspati** (same as Jupiter): Known as the celestial preceptor and teacher of the gods in Hindu mythology, Brihaspati symbolizes wisdom, intellect, and spiritual guidance. He is the deity of Jupiter, embodying growth,

prosperity, and ethical living. Revered as the ultimate guru, Brihaspati inspires seekers to pursue higher knowledge and align with the principles of dharma.

10. **Chyavana (ch-yah-vah-nah)**: An ancient sage from Hindu mythology who underwent transformation and healing by the Ashwini Kumaras, representing renewal and trust in divine guidance.
11. **Cosmic Message**: Spiritual wisdom derived from celestial energies, providing guidance for self-awareness and growth.
12. **Daksha (duck-shah)**: A progenitor in Hindu mythology and father of the 27 Nakshatras. Known for his pivotal role in mythological stories, including conflicts with Shiva.
13. **Devas (day-vahs)**: Celestial beings in Hindu mythology, representing positive and benevolent forces in the cosmos.
14. **Dharma**: A foundational concept in Indian philosophy, Dharma signifies the moral order, duty, and purpose that sustains the universe and human life. It embodies the principles of righteousness, guiding individuals to live in harmony with their true nature, societal roles, and cosmic laws. Dharma is not a rigid rule but a dynamic path, unique to each person, meant to align their actions with higher truths and collective well-being.
15. **Gautama**: is a revered sage in Vedic and Hindu traditions, known for his profound wisdom and contributions to spiritual and philosophical teachings. Often associated with the lineage of great rishis, Gautama represents the quest for truth and understanding, embodying the principles of dharma and ascetic discipline. He is also known for his role in the story of Ahalya, where themes of redemption and forgiveness are explored.
16. **Halahala**: In Hindu mythology, *halahala* is the deadly poison that emerged during the churning of the ocean (Samudra Manthan) by the gods (Devas) and demons (Asuras). Its destructive power was so immense that it threatened to consume all creation. Lord Shiva, out of compassion, drank the poison to protect the universe, holding it in his throat, which turned blue, earning him

the name **Neelkantha** (the blue-throated one). Halahala symbolizes overwhelming challenges or toxic influences that, when addressed with courage and self-sacrifice, can lead to transformation and balance.

17. **Indra (in-drah)**: The king of the gods in Hindu mythology, associated with rain, storms, and protection. Indra symbolizes power and cosmic balance.
18. **Kamadhenu (kah-mah-day-noo)**: A divine, wish-fulfilling cow in Hindu mythology, symbolizing abundance, fertility, and prosperity. Kamadhenu is often regarded as the source of all nourishment and a sacred being.
19. **Kailash (kye-lahsh)**: Mount Kailash, considered the abode of Lord Shiva, symbolic of spiritual enlightenment and liberation.
20. **Kartikeya (kart-tih-kay-yah)**: A warrior deity and son of Shiva, associated with courage, precision, and overcoming illusions. Also called Skanda or Murugan, he represents divine victory over chaos.
21. **Kosala (koh-sah-lah)**: An ancient and prosperous kingdom in Indian mythology, often associated with the city of Ayodhya. Kosala is the birthplace of Lord Rama, as described in the epic *Ramayana*, and symbolizes righteousness and cultural heritage.
22. **Krishna (krish-nah)**: A central deity in Hinduism, revered as the eighth avatar of Vishnu. Krishna embodies divine love, wisdom, and playful transcendence, often depicted in the Bhagavad Gita as a guide to Arjuna on the battlefield of Kurukshetra.
23. **Mandara Mountain (man-dah-rah)**: A mountain used as a churning rod in the Samudra Manthan story as per myths.
24. **Maya (mah-yah)**: The concept of illusion in Indian philosophy, describing the veil that obscures reality and binds beings to the material world.
25. **Mriga (Deer) (mree-guh)**: A symbolic deer in Vedic mythology, representing the quest for self-realization and truth. It is central to Rudra's story in the Mrigashira

Nakshatra.

26. **Nakshatra (nuhk-shuh-tra)**: Lunar mansions or constellations in Vedic astrology dividing the moon's orbit into 27 segments.

27. **Naga (Serpent) (nah-gah)**: Mystical serpents in Hindu mythology, representing wisdom, power, and spiritual transformation.

28. **Narada (nah-rah-dah)**: A divine sage in Hindu mythology, known as a celestial messenger and musician. Narada is revered for his wisdom, devotion, and role as a cosmic mediator, often appearing in myths to provide guidance or provoke events that lead to greater spiritual understanding. He is also associated with the veena (a musical instrument) and is considered a devotee of Lord Vishnu.

29. **Neelkanth (neel-kunth)**: A name for Lord Shiva, referring to his blue throat, which he acquired after consuming poison during the churning of the ocean.

30. **Pitri (pit-ree)**: The ancestors or spirits of departed souls, revered in Vedic tradition for their guidance and blessings.

31. **Radha (rah-dhah)**: Krishna's beloved and an embodiment of devotion and unconditional love in Hindu mythology. Radha represents the soul's longing and ultimate union with the divine.

32. **Raghu (ruh-goo)**: A legendary king of the Ikshvaku dynasty in Hindu mythology, known for his valor, generosity, and adherence to dharma (cosmic law). The term "Raghuvansha" (Raghu's lineage) refers to the royal lineage of Lord Rama, celebrated in Kalidasa's epic poem *Raghuvansha*.

33. **Rahu (rah-hoo)**: A shadow planet in Vedic astrology representing desires, illusions, and karmic challenges.

34. **Ramayana (rah-mah-yuh-nah)**: One of the two greatest Hindu epics, narrating the life and adventures of Lord Rama. (**Rama** is the central character of the Indian epic *Ramayana*, revered as the seventh avatar of the Hindu god Vishnu. Known as **Maryada Purushottama** (the Perfect Man), Rama embodies virtues like righteousness, duty, compassion, and honor. His life and journey represent the

ideal path of dharma (righteousness) in human existence. His story revolves around his exile, the abduction of his wife Sita by Ravana, the battle to rescue her, and his eventual return to Ayodhya to establish a golden era of justice and prosperity.)

35. **Rudra (roo-drah)**: A fierce form of Shiva in Hindu mythology, representing destruction and transformation.
36. **Sacred Transition**: A transformative phase in life or spirituality that signifies moving from one state of being to a higher level of understanding or existence.
37. **Samudra Manthan (suh-moo-drah man-than)** : The cosmic churning of the ocean in Hindu mythology, symbolizing balance between opposing forces.
38. **Sarayu River (sah-rah-yoo)**: A sacred river in India, often mentioned in Hindu texts like the Ramayana, associated with purification and sanctity.
39. **Shakti (shuhk-tee)**: The divine feminine energy or power that drives creation, destruction, and transformation in Vedic cosmology.
40. **Shesha (Sheshanag) (shay-shah)**: The cosmic serpent in Hindu mythology who balances the universe on its coils, symbolizing stability and infinity.
41. **Shiva**: One of the principal deities in Hinduism, Shiva is known as the destroyer and transformer within the cosmic trinity (Trimurti). Representing the balance between creation, preservation, and destruction, he embodies the cycles of life and renewal. Often depicted meditating on Mount Kailash or as the cosmic dancer Nataraja, Shiva symbolizes ultimate awareness, liberation, and the power to transcend illusions.
42. **Soma (soh-mah)**: The Vedic deity of the Moon, symbolizing nourishment, vitality, and emotional rhythm.
43. **Tarakasura (tah-rah-kah-soo-rah)**: A demon in Hindu mythology defeated by Kartikeya, representing illusions and challenges that test one's clarity.
44. **Varanasi** (aka Kashi aka Banaras): Varanasi, often called the spiritual heart of India, stands as one of the world's oldest continuously inhabited cities. Situated along the

sacred Ganges (Ganga) River, it holds a unique place as a revered center of Hinduism and spirituality. For thousands of years, Varanasi has been a hub for rituals, philosophy, and the arts, drawing seekers from across the globe to its timeless energy. The city's iconic ghats (riverfront steps) come alive with the rhythm of life—from serene pre-dawn prayers to sacred cremation ceremonies, resonating with music, meditation, and devotion. For millions of followers of Hinduism and Sanatan Dharma, it is a pilgrimage destination like no other. Adding to its mystique, Varanasi is uniquely located at a point where the mighty Ganges takes a rare south-to-north turn. This phenomenon is believed to alter the river's magnetic properties, giving Ganga Jal (the water of the Ganges) special spiritual significance. Nestled within Varanasi is Sarnath, the sacred site where Gautama Buddha delivered his first sermon after enlightenment.

45. **Varuna:** is the Vedic deity of cosmic order and the oceans, embodying truth, justice, and the universal laws that govern existence. Known as the upholder of ṛta (cosmic order), he watches over moral conduct and symbolizes the balance between the seen and unseen worlds.
46. **Vasishtha (vah-sish-thah)**: One of the revered seven sages (Saptarishis) in Hindu tradition, known as a great teacher, philosopher, and spiritual guide. Vasishtha was the royal teacher of the Raghu dynasty and played a significant role in the education of Lord Rama. He is also credited with composing parts of the *Rigveda*.
47. **Vasu**: In Vedic tradition, the Vasus are a group of eight elemental deities representing natural phenomena like fire, water, wind, and earth. They are known as the attendants of Indra and Vishnu, embodying the foundational energies that sustain life and creation. In mythology, their stories often symbolize the interplay of duty, cosmic balance, and the eternal nature of the soul.
48. **Vasuki (vah-soo-kee)**: The king of serpents in Hindu mythology, often depicted in the cosmic churning story (Samudra Manthan).

49. **Vedic Astrology (Jyotisha)**: An ancient Indian system of astrology based on celestial bodies' movements to interpret their effects on human life.
50. **Vishnu (vish-noo)**: A major deity in Hinduism, the Preserver and Operator of the universe who maintains cosmic balance.
51. **Vishwakarma (vish-wah-kar-mah)**: The divine architect in Vedic mythology responsible for creating celestial weapons, palaces, and tools.
52. **Yajna (Yagna) (yuhg-nuh)**: A sacred fire ritual in Hinduism, symbolizing devotion, purification, and the connection between humans and the divine.
53. **Yama (yah-mah)**: The Hindu god of death and justice, ensuring the proper balance of life and guiding souls through rebirth cycles.
54. **Yoni (yo-nee)**: A sacred symbol in Vedic tradition, Yoni represents the source of creation, fertility, and the divine feminine energy. Often depicted as a cosmic womb or the vagina, it signifies the cyclical nature of life, renewal, and the interconnectedness of all existence. In spiritual contexts, it is a reminder of the balance between creation and sustenance in the universe.

<u>Author's Note on Varanasi</u>: *Although I was born in this city, I only visited during vacations. I despised the place as a child. I had seen several uncouth people and came across many 'men of god' who were there only to fleece. The dirt and the stench of the place back then, did not help either. Until once, during my early teens, when our train was approaching the city, crossing the bridge over the Ganga river, I felt a strange pull. An amazing vibe which has never left me. Many years later, it struck me that if Shiva himself drank poison to save the universe, how could his city be free from toxins? A place as magnetic as this had to attract the deprived souls as well. Ever since, I have come to 'feel' that this city is like a portal. I am still unsure what kind of portal. Whether it connects the soul to someplace special or brings in divine realizations to the earth from somewhere, is not clear to me, yet. But I have felt this. And my respect for this place is now infinite. I would encourage readers to go to Varanasi and visit places which are not driven by materialism. Spend some time there in peace, and you might feel the magic too.*

List of 27 Nakshatras (aka constellations, aka Lunar Mansions) with their pronunciations:

1. Ashwini (ush-win-ee)
2. Bharani (buh-rah-nee)
3. Krittika (krit-tih-kah)
4. Rohini (roh-hee-nee)
5. Mrigashira (mree-guh-shee-rah)
6. Ardra (ahr-drah)
7. Punarvasu (poo-nahr-vah-soo)
8. Pushya (push-yah)
9. Ashlesha (ush-lay-shah)
10. Magha (muh-ghah)
11. Purva Phalguni (poor-vah fahl-goo-nee)
12. Uttara Phalguni (oot-tah-rah fahl-goo-nee)
13. Hasta (hus-tah)
14. Chitra (chit-rah)
15. Swati (swah-tee)
16. Vishakha (vish-ah-kah)
17. Anuradha (uh-noo-rah-dhah)
18. Jyeshtha (jay-shthah)
19. Moola (moo-lah)
20. Purva Ashadha (poor-vah ush-ah-dhah)
21. Uttara Ashadha (oot-tah-rah ush-ah-dhah)
22. Shravana (shruh-vah-nah)
23. Dhanishta (dhuh-nee-sh-tah)
24. Shatabhisha (shuh-tah-bee-shah)
25. Purva Bhadrapada (poor-vah bhuh-drah-pah-dah)
26. Uttara Bhadrapada (oot-tah-rah bhuh-drah-pah-dah)
27. Revati (ray-vah-tee)

List of Lunar Mansions, Zodiacs and Ownerships

Nakshatra	Its Ruler	Zodiac Sign	Zodiac Ruler
Ashwini	Ketu	Aries	Mars
Bharani	Venus	Aries	Mars
Krittika	Sun	Aries/Taurus	Mars/Venus
Rohini	Moon	Taurus	Venus
Mrigashira	Mars	Taurus/Gemini	Venus/ Mercury
Ardra	Rahu	Gemini	Mercury
Punarvasu	Jupiter	Gemini/Cancer	Moon
Pushya	Saturn	Cancer	Moon
Ashlesha	Mercury	Cancer	Moon
Magha	Ketu	Leo	Sun
Purva Phalguni	Venus	Leo	Sun
Uttara Phalguni	Sun	Leo/Virgo	Sun/Mercury
Hasta	Moon	Virgo	Mercury
Chitra	Mars	Virgo/Libra	Mercury/ Venus
Swati	Rahu	Libra	Venus
Vishakha	Jupiter	Libra/Scorpio	Venus/Mars
Anuradha	Saturn	Scorpio	Mars
Jyeshtha	Mercury	Scorpio	Mars
Moola	Ketu	Sagittarius	Jupiter
Purva Ashadha	Venus	Sagittarius	Jupiter

Uttara Ashadha	Sun	Sagittarius/ Capricorn	Jupiter/Saturn
Shravana	Moon	Capricorn	Saturn
Dhanishta	Mars	Capricorn/ Aquarius	Saturn
Shatabhisha	Rahu	Aquarius	Saturn
Purva Bhadrapada	Jupiter	Aquarius/Pisces	Saturn/Jupiter
Uttara Bhadrapada	Saturn	Pisces	Jupiter
Revati	Mercury	Pisces	Jupiter

Planets as per Vedic Astrology and Attributes they impart

Planets	Attributes
Sun	Authority, vitality, self-expression, leadership
Moon	Emotions, mind, intuition, nurturing
Mars	Energy, courage, determination, action
Mercury	Intellect, communication, adaptability, business acumen
Jupiter	Wisdom, spirituality, growth, prosperity
Venus	Love, beauty, relationships, creativity
Saturn	Discipline, structure, perseverance, responsibility
Rahu	Ambition, illusion, innovation, material desires
Ketu	Detachment, spirituality, enlightenment, karmic lessons

BOOKS BY THIS AUTHOR

Cracking Rahu: Navigating Desire, Fomo And Chaos

Rahu (North Node) is said to be the driving force behind modern desires, ambition, and digital chaos in astrology. But Cracking Rahu: Navigating Desire, FOMO and Chaos isn't about diving into astrological charts—it's about life, told through a tale of humor, heart, and deeply relatable insights into the forces shaping us.

This book offers a fresh, engaging exploration of spirituality and astrology intertwined with the messy, beautiful realities of modern living.

Meet Neel, a tech-savvy dreamer escaping into virtual worlds after his startup's failure, and Arya, his girlfriend and a professor, striving to close the emotional distance between them. Alongside them are Shaan, their charming yet conflicted friend navigating love and identity, and NV, a wise mentor whose cosmic insights cut through the chaos.

Through these stories, the book examines ambition, love, escapism, and self-discovery, framed by Rahu—the cosmic force of illusion and relentless drive—and the challenges of Kaal Sarpa Dosha.

Cracking Rahu (by the same author)

Scan for More info on Author books and resources

ABOUT THE AUTHOR

Nitin Vasishtha

A corporate leader for over 2 decades, turned wisdom miner, offers a multidimensional perspective on personal growth and transformation. Born into a lineage of spiritual seekers in Varanasi, India, he built a successful career in engineering, business management, and entrepreneurship while deeply immersing himself in the study of astrology, spirituality, and human psychology. His diverse life experiences, spanning multiple geographies and languages, have profoundly shaped his unique approach to guiding individuals on their personal journeys.

Despite his professional achievements, Nitin struggled with the elusiveness of true peace—a realisation that strengthened his commitment to helping others navigate their own paths of transformation. Since 1996, he has been bridging the gap between ancient wisdom and modern living. As an astrologer, life-purpose and relationship counselor, CrossFit enthusiast, Ultra-marathon runner, and advocate of biohacking, Nitin integrates holistic wellness with personal empowerment in his work.

His debut books, 'Constellations Within' and 'Cracking Rahu', draw on the wisdom of the ancient sciences, offering practical insights to align one's will and efforts for positive growth. Through relatable storytelling and profound guidance, Nitin inspires readers to confront their struggles, reassess their journeys, and uncover clarity amidst life's uncertainties.

When he's not writing or engaging with inquisitive minds, Nitin enjoys spending time with his dog, Yaara, or delving into the intersections of self-awareness, free will, and the human spirit. He currently lives in Bangalore, India, with his wife and daughter. He can be reached @mining.wisdom on Insta

www.ingramcontent.com/pod-product-compliance
Lightning Source LLC
Chambersburg PA
CBHW062134160726
48282CB00027B/819
9788198052995